Photo by David Zeiger

A scene from the Alliance Theatre Company production of "Flyin' West." Set design by Dex Edwards.

FLYIN' WEST
WEST
BY PEARL CLEAGE

DRAMATISTS
PLAY SERVICE
INC.

2

FLYIN' WEST was originally commissioned and produced by Alliance Theatre Company (Kenny Leon, Artistic Director; Edith Love, Managing Director), in Atlanta, Georgia, in association with AT&T: On Stage, in November, 1992. It was directed by Kenny Leon; the set design was by Dex Edwards; the lighting design was by P. Hamilton Shinn; the costume design was by Jeff Cone and the musical composition was by Dwight Andrews. The cast was as follows:

SOPHIE WASHINGTON .... Sharlene Ross
MISS LEAH .... Carol Mitchell-Leon
FANNIE DOVE .... Elizabeth Van Dyke
WIL PARISH .... Donald Griffin
MINNIE DOVE CHARLES .... Kimberly Hawthorne
FRANK CHARLES .... Peter Jay Fernandez

CHARACTERS

SOPHIE WASHINGTON — a black woman, born into slavery, age 36
MISS LEAH — a black woman, born into slavery, age 73
FANNIE DOVE — a black woman, age 32
WIL PARISH — a black man, born into slavery, age 40
MINNIE DOVE CHARLES — a black woman, age 21
FRANK CHARLES — a very light skinned black man, born into slavery, age 36

TIME

Fall, 1898.

PLACE

Outside the all-black town of Nicodemus, Kansas.

SETTING

The play takes place in and around the house shared by Sophie, Fannie and, more recently, Miss Leah. The women are wheat farmers and the house sits in the midst of the vastness of the Kansas prairie. Activity will take place mainly in the house's kitchen/dining/living room, which has a table, chairs, a small desk, a wood-burning stove, etc. In the back and upstairs are other bedrooms, one of which will also be the scene of action during the play. Other activities takes place in the area outside the front door, including wood gathering and chopping, hanging of clothes to dry, etc. There is also a brief arrival scene at the nearby train station, which need only be suggested.

ACT ONE
Scene 1 — A fall evening
Scene 2 — Two days later; early afternoon
Scene 3 — The same day; evening
Scene 4 — The next morning
Scene 5 — Late that night

ACT TWO
Scene 1 — Early the next morning
Scene 2 — The next Sunday; early morning
Scene 3 — Sunday afternoon
Scene 4 — Sunday evening
Scene 5 — Monday morning
Scene 6 — Seven months later; April, 1899

AUTHOR'S NOTES

The Homestead Act of 1860 offered 320 acres of "free" land stolen from the dwindling populations of Native Americans, to U.S. citizens who were willing to settle in the western states. Although many settlers lived in traditional family groups, by 1890, a quarter of a million unmarried or widowed women were running their own farms and ranches. The farm work was hard and constant, but many of these women were able to survive due to their own physical stamina, determination and the help of their neighbors.

Large groups of African American homesteaders left the South following the Civil War to settle all-black towns. The so-called "Exodus of 1879" saw twenty to forty-thousand African American men, women and children — "Exodusters" — reach Kansas under the guidance of a charismatic leader, Benjamin "Pap" Singleton, who escaped from slavery and claimed later, "I am the whole cause of the Kansas migration!"

Crusading black journalist Ida B. Wells' call to her readers to leave Memphis, Tennessee, after an 1892 lynching and riot, was heeded by over 7,000 black residents of the city who packed up as many of their belongings as they could carry and headed west in search of a life free from racist violence. Unfortunately their dreams were shattered as many Western states enacted Jim Crow laws as cruel as any in the old Confederacy and effectively destroyed most of the black settlements by the early 1900s.

This is a story of some of the black people who went West.

FLYIN' WEST

ACT ONE

Scene 1

Sophie enters rapidly. Her heavy coat is unbuttoned and her scarf flies out around her neck. It is chilly, but the cold has exhilarated her. She has just returned from a trip into town. She has a large bag of flour slung over her shoulder and a canvas shoulder bag full of groceries. She is carrying a shotgun, which she places by the door. She slings the bag of flour carelessly on the table and, coat still on, puts the other bag on a chair. She fumbles through her pockets, first withdrawing a letter, which she holds for a moment thoughtfully, then sticks in the growing pile on the overflowing desk. She fumbles through her pockets again and withdraws some long strips of black licorice. She takes a bite, sighs, chews appreciatively. She pulls a chair over to the window, opens it wide and sits down, propping her booted feet up on the window sill. She looks out the window with great contentment, takes another bite of licorice and chews slowly, completely satisfied with the candy's sweetness, the chill in the air and the privacy of the moment.

Miss Leah enters haltingly. She walks unsteadily but has no cane to steady herself, so she holds onto the furniture as she walks slowly into the room. She is looking for something and her manner is exasperated. Sophie does not notice her entering. Miss Leah looks at Sophie, immediately notices the open window and her irritation increases.

7

MISS LEAH.   Well, ain't you somethin'!

SOPHIE.   I didn't know you were up, Miss Leah. Want a piece? *(Sophie gets up and closes the window, stokes the fire, etc.)*

MISS LEAH.   I hate licorice. *(Miss Leah stumbles a little. Sophie moves to steady her and is stopped by a "don't you dare" look from Miss Leah.)*

SOPHIE.   You miss your cane?

MISS LEAH.   I don't need no cane! I told you that before. You can lay it next to my bed or prop it against my chair like it walked out there on its own. It still ain't gonna make me no never mind. I don't want no cane and I don't need no cane.

SOPHIE.   Suit yourself. *(Takes another bite of licorice as she hangs her coat. Miss Leah's shawl is hanging there in plain view. Sophie starts to reach for it, stops, ignores it and begins putting things away. Miss Leah finally speaks with cold dignity.)*

MISS LEAH.   I am looking for my shawl, if you must know.

SOPHIE.   It's right ...

MISS LEAH.   Don't tell me! If you start tellin' me, you'll just keep at it 'til I won't be able to remember a darn thing on my own.

SOPHIE.   I'll make some coffee.

MISS LEAH.   I don't know why. Can't nobody drink that stuff but you.

SOPHIE.   It'll warm you up.

MISS LEAH.   It'll kill me.

SOPHIE.   Well, then, you haven't got much time to put your affairs in order.

MISS LEAH.   My affairs are already in order, thank you. *(Pulls her chair as far from the window as possible and sits with effort.)* It's too cold for first October. *(Shivering.)* Where's my shawl? Don't tell me!

SOPHIE.   I bought you some tobacco.

MISS LEAH.   What kind?

SOPHIE.   The kind you like.

MISS LEAH.   *(Pleased in spite of herself.)* Well, thank you, Sister Sophie. Maybe a good pipe can cut the taste of that mess you cookin' up in Fan's good coffee pot. *(She proceeds to make a pipe while Sophie makes coffee.)* What are we celebrating?

SOPHIE.   We are celebrating my ability not to let these Nicodemus Negroes worry me, no matter how hard they try.

MISS LEAH.   Then we ought to be drinking corn whiskey. *(Miss Leah lights the pipe and draws on it contentedly.)* Are you still worrying about the vote?

SOPHIE.   I just told you. I'm celebrating an end to worrying. *(A beat.)* I rode in by way of the south ridge this morning. Smells like snow up there already.

MISS LEAH.   What were you doing way over there?

SOPHIE.   Just looking ...

MISS LEAH.   Ain't you got enough land to worry about?

SOPHIE.   I'll have enough when I can step outside my door and spin around with my eyes closed and wherever I stop, as far as I can see, there'll be nothing but land that belongs to me and my sisters.

MISS LEAH.   Well, I'll try not to let the smoke from my chimney drift out over your sky.

SOPHIE.   That's very neighborly of you. Now drink some of this.

MISS LEAH.   *(Drinks and grimaces.)* Every other wagon pull in here nowadays got a bunch of colored women on it call themselves homesteadin' and can't even make a decent cup of coffee, much less bring a crop in! When I got here, it wadn't nobody to do nothin' for me but me ....

TOGETHER.   ... and I did everything there was to be done and then some ...

MISS LEAH.   That's right! Because I was not prepared to put up with a whole lotta mouth. Colored men always tryin' to tell you how to do somethin' even if you been doin' it longer than they been peein' standin' up. *(A beat.)* They got that in common with you.

SOPHIE.   I don't pee standing up.

MISS LEAH.   You would if you could! *(Sips coffee and grimaces again.)*

SOPHIE.   Put some milk in it, Miss Leah.

MISS LEAH.   When I want milk, I drink milk. When I want coffee, I want Fan's coffee!

SOPHIE.   Suit yourself. *(A beat.)* People were asking about Baker at the land office.

MISS LEAH.   What people?

SOPHIE.   White people. Asked me if I had heard anything from him.

MISS LEAH.   Ain't no white folks looking to settle in no Nicodemus, Kansas.

SOPHIE.   It's some of the best land around here. You said it yourself.

MISS LEAH.   Ain't nothin' good to no white folks once a bunch of colored folks get set up on it!

SOPHIE.   There's already a new family over by the Gaddy's and a widower with four sons between here and the Jordan place. They've probably been looking at your place, too.

MISS LEAH.   Who said so?

SOPHIE.   Nobody said anything. I just mean since you've been staying with us for a while.

MISS LEAH.   Well, I ain't no wet behind the ears home-steader. I own my land. Free and clear. My name the only name on the deed to it. Anybody lookin' at my land is countin' they chickens. I made twenty winters on that land and I intend to make twenty more. *(While Miss Leah fusses, Sophie quietly goes and gets her shawl and gently drops it around her shoulders.)*

SOPHIE.   And then what?

MISS LEAH.   Then maybe I'll let you have it.

SOPHIE.   You gonna make me wait until I'm old as you are to get my hands on your orchard?

MISS LEAH.   That'll be time enough. If I tell you you can have it any sooner, my life won't be worth two cents!

SOPHIE.   You don't really think I'd murder you for your land, do you? *(Miss Leah looks at Sophie for a beat before drawing deeply on her pipe.)*

MISS LEAH.   I like Baker. And Miz Baker sweet as she can be. They just tryin' to stay in the city long enough for her to get her strength back and build that baby up a little.

SOPHIE.   She'll never make it out here and you know it.

MISS LEAH.   Losing three babies in three years take it out

of you, girl!

SOPHIE.   They wouldn't have made it through the first winter if Wil Parrish hadn't been here to help them.

MISS LEAH.   You had a lot of help your first coupla winters, if I remember it right.

SOPHIE.   And I'm grateful for it.

MISS LEAH.   Some of us were here when you got here. Don't forget it!

SOPHIE.   All I'm trying to say is the Bakers have been gone almost two years and he hasn't even filed an extension. It's against the rules.

MISS LEAH.   Against whose rules? Don't nobody but colored folks know they been gone that long no way. Them white folks never come out here to even check and see if we're dead or alive. You know that good as the next person. *(A beat.)* Sometimes I suspect you think you the only one love this land, Sister, but you not.

SOPHIE.   What are you getting at?

MISS LEAH.   Just the way you were speechifyin' and carryin' on in town meetin' last week like you the only one got a opinion that matter.

SOPHIE.   Why didn't the others speak up if they had so much to say?

MISS LEAH.   Can't get a word in edgewise with you goin' on and on about who ain't doin' this and that like they 'spose to.

SOPHIE.   But you know I'm right!

MISS LEAH.   Bein' right ain't always the only thing you got to think about. The thing you gotta remember about colored folks is all the stuff they don't say when they want to, they just gonna say it double time later. That's why you gonna lose that vote if you ain't careful.

SOPHIE.   It doesn't make sense. A lot of the colored settlements have already passed rules saying nobody can sell to outsiders unless everybody agrees.

MISS LEAH.   Ain't nobody gonna give you the right to tell them when and how to sell their land. No point in ownin' it if you can't do what you want to with it.

SOPHIE.   But half of them will sell to the speculators! You know they will!

MISS LEAH.   Then that's what they gonna have to do.

SOPHIE.   We could have so much here if these colored folks would just step lively. We could own this whole prairie. Nothing but colored folks farms and colored folks wheat fields and colored folks cattle everywhere you look. Nothing but colored folks! But they can't see it. They look at Nicodemus and all they can see is a bunch of scuffling people trying to get ready for the winter instead of something free and fine and all our own. Most of them don't even know what we're doing here!

MISS LEAH.   That's 'cause some of them come 'cause they ain't never had nothin' that belonged to 'em. Some of them come 'cause they can't stand the smell of the city. Some of them just tired of evil white folks. Some of 'em killed somebody or wanted to. All everybody got in common is they plunked down twelve dollars for a piece of good land and now they tryin' to live on it long enough to claim it.

SOPHIE.   Everybody isn't even doing that.

MISS LEAH.   Everybody doin' the best they can, Sister Sophie.

SOPHIE.   And what happens when that isn't good enough?

MISS LEAH.   Then they have to drink your coffee! *(Sophie laughs as Wil and Fannie enter outside. We can still see the activity in the house, but we no longer hear it. Miss Leah is smoking her pipe and Sophie is working on her ledgers at the messy desk. She pushes Fannie's papers aside carelessly, completely focused. Wil is dressed in work clothes. Fannie is dressed in boots, long skirt, shawl. They are strolling companionably and chatting with the ease of old and trusted friends.)*

WIL.   I guess I'd have to say the weather more than anything. I miss that Mexican sunshine. Makes everything warm. You know how cold these creeks are when you want to take a swim? Well, I like to swim bein' from Florida and all, so I close my eyes and jump in real quick! But that water would neigh 'bout kill a Mexican. They don't know nothin' 'bout no cold. They even eat their food hot! *(Fannie, laughing, stops to pick a flower to add to her already overflowing basket.)*

FANNIE. Look! *(Holding it up for Wil's inspection.)* That'll be the last of these until spring.

WIL. I imagine it will be. I ate a Mexican hot pepper one time. It looked just like a Louisiana hot pepper, but when I bit into it, it neigh 'bout lifted the top of my head off. Them Mexicans were laughing so hard they couldn't even bring me no water. I like to died!

FANNIE. You really miss it, don't you?

WIL. Miss Fannie, sometimes I surely do. But I know Baker needs somebody to keep an eye on things for him until he gets back. And now I got Miss Leah's place to look in on too.

FANNIE. Do you think they'll be back this spring?

WIL. He swears they will.

FANNIE. Sophie doesn't think they're strong enough for this life.

WIL. Sometimes people are a lot stronger then you can tell by just lookin' at 'em.

FANNIE. Did he say anything about the baby?

WIL. Said he's fat and healthy and looks just like him, poor little thing!

FANNIE. *(Laughing.)* Shame on you! *(A beat.)* Has Miss Leah said anything to you about going home?

WIL. No. Not lately.

FANNIE. Good! We're trying to convince her to stay the winter with us.

WIL. She's not tryin' to go back to her place alone, is she?

FANNIE. She really wants to, but she's just gotten so frail. Sophie says it was just a matter of time before she fell and broke something.

WIL. *(A beat.)* You know what else I like? I mean about Mexico?

FANNIE. What?

WIL. I like Mexicans.

FANNIE. Well, that works out nice, I guess.

WIL. Everybody livin' in Mexico don't like Mexicans, Miss Fannie. They separate out the people from the stuff they do like and go on about their business like they ain't even there.

FANNIE. I never met any Mexicans.

WIL. Nicest people you ever wanna see. Friendly, but know how to keep to they self, too. Didn't no Mexicans ever say nothin' out of the way to me as long as I was livin' down there. They a lot like them Seminoles I grew up around in Florida. When I run away, them Indians took me in and raised me up like I was one of their own. They most all gone now. Ain't got enough land left to spit on, if you'll forgive me sayin' it that way.

FANNIE. Do you think you'll go back? To Mexico, I mean.

WIL. I used to think so but I spent seven years down there. As long as I spent on anybody's plantation, so I guess I'm back even. *(A beat.)* I might even be a little bit ahead. *(He hands her a flower that has fallen out of her basket.)*

FANNIE. *(Embarrassed.)* My mother loved flowers. Roses were her favorites. My father used to say, "colored women ain't got no time to be foolin' with no roses" and my mother would say, as long as colored men had time to worry about how colored women spent their time, she guessed she had time enough to grow some roses.

WIL. I like sunflowers. They got sunflowers in Mexico big as a plate.

FANNIE. Sophie likes sunflowers, too, but they're too big to put inside the house. They belong outside. *(A beat.)* It's lonely out here without flowers. Sophie laughed the first time everything I planted around the house came into bloom. She said I had planted so many flowers there wasn't any room for the beans and tomatoes.

WIL. That's where your sister's wrong. There's room for everything to grow out here. If there ain't nothin' else out here, there's plenty of room. *(They stand together, looking at the beauty of the sunset. Wil turns after a moment and looks at her, quietly removing his hat and holding it nervously in his hands.)*

FANNIE. You think it's going to a long winter, Wil?

WIL. They're all long winters, Miss Fannie. This one will be about the same.

FANNIE. Sophie found her laugh out here. I don't remember ever hearing her laugh the whole time we were in Memphis. But everything in Kansas was funny to her. Sometimes when we first got here, she'd laugh so hard she'd start cry-ing, but she didn't care. One time, she was laughing so hard I was afraid she was going to have a stroke. She scared me to death. When she calmed down, I asked her well, why didn't you ever laugh like that in Memphis? And she said her laugh was too free to come out in a place where a colored woman's life wasn't worth two cents on the dollar. What kind of fool would find that funny, she asked me. She was right, too. Sophie's always right. *(While she speaks, Wil reaches out very slowly and almost puts his arm around her waist. She does not see him and he stops before touching her, suddenly terrified she would not appreci-ate the gesture. She picks up the flowers and hesitates.)* We're friends, aren't we?

WIL.   Yes, Miss Fannie. I would say we are.

FANNIE.   Then I wish you'd just call me Fannie. You don't have to called me Miss Fannie.

WIL.   *(Embarrassed.)* I didn't mean to offend you, Miss ... I just sort of like to call you that because it reminds me that a colored women is a precious jewel deserving of my respect, my love and my protection.

FANNIE.   *(Taken aback and delighted.)* Why, Wil! What a sweet thing to say!

WIL.   My mother taught it to me. She used to make me say it at night like other folks said prayers. There were some other things she said, too, but I can't remember them anymore. When I first run off after they sold her, I tried to close my eyes and remember her voice sayin' 'em, but all them new In-dian words was lookin' for a place in my head, too. So I lost 'em all but that one I just told you. She used to say if a col-ored man could just remember that one thing, life would be a whole lot easier on the colored woman.

FANNIE.   Can I put it in the book?

WIL.   With Miss Leah's stories?

FANNIE.   It's not just Miss Leah's stories anymore, Wil. It's sort of about all of us.

WIL.   I would call it an honor to be included.

FANNIE.   Well, good! *(Suddenly embarrassed, she adjusts her shawl and prepares to go inside.)*

WIL.   Walkin' with you has been the pleasure of my day.
FANNIE.   Would you like some coffee before you start back?
WIL.   No, thanks. I want to catch the last of the light. Give
my best to your sister.
FANNIE.   I will.
WIL.   And Miss Leah.
FANNIE.   Yes, I will.
WIL.   Tell her ... Miss Leah ... maybe I'll stop in ... tomor-
row?
FANNIE.   We'll look for you.
WIL.   Well, good evening then.
FANNIE.   Good evening. *(He starts off. Miss Leah comes to the
window and watches the parting.)* Wil ... *(He turns back hopefully.
Fannie walks to him and puts a flower in his button hole.)* Take
this for company on your way back.
WIL.   Why, thank you! I do thank you.
FANNIE.   Good evening, Wil.
WIL.   And to you ... Miss Fannie. *(He tips his hat and walks
off, adjusting the flower in his button hole. Fannie watches him un-
til he is gone, then walks slowly to the house. Miss Leah returns to
her seat and begins humming "Amazing Grace." Sophie looks at her.
She continues humming loudly and rocking with a smug look on her
face.)*
SOPHIE.   What is it?
MISS LEAH.   I ain't said a word to you.
SOPHIE.   You're humming at me!
MISS LEAH.   I ain't hummin' at nobody. I am just hummin'.
(Fannie enters with flowers.)
FANNIE.   I'm sorry to be so late!
MISS LEAH.   Sophie made coffee.
SOPHIE.   She's been humming at me ever since. *(Fannie kisses
Sophie's cheek and pats Miss Leah.)*
FANNIE.   Everything is fine at your place, Miss Leah. *(She
puts the flowers in water and arranges them quickly around the room.)*
MISS LEAH.   Everythin's fine but me.
FANNIE.   Aren't you feeling good?
MISS LEAH.   I'm too old to feel good. How's Wil Parrish
feelin'?

FANNIE.   He's just fine, thank you.
SOPHIE.   Did he walk back with you? Why didn't he come in?
FANNIE.   He'll be by tomorrow.
SOPHIE.   You should have invited Wil Parrish in for a cup of coffee.
FANNIE.   I did. He wanted to catch the last light.
MISS LEAH.   Well, that sure was a friendly flower you stuck in his button hole a few minutes ago! But it's none of my business. *(Starts humming again.)*
FANNIE.   I ran into him watering his horse near the creek and he walked back with me. That's all.
SOPHIE.   Has he heard from Baker?
FANNIE.   He had a letter last week. Mother and baby are both doing fine.
SOPHIE.   There's some people interested in that land.
FANNIE.   Who?
SOPHIE.   Families. White families.
FANNIE.   In Nicodemus?
MISS LEAH.   Just what I said!
FANNIE.   I don't believe it. All the settlements they've got, why would they want to file a claim over here with us?
SOPHIE.   Why don't you ask some of those land speculators holed up at the boarding house? *(The food is laid out and they seat themselves. Sophie moves to help Miss Leah who waves her away and will only accept help from Fannie.)*
FANNIE.   Well, it's neither here nor there. They'll be back on that land themselves by spring.
SOPHIE.   I hope so. I don't need a whole bunch of strange white folks living that close to me! *(They are seated and Fannie lights a candle in the center of the table. The three join hands.)*
FANNIE.   Bless this food, oh Lord, we are about to receive for the nourishment of our bodies, through Jesus Christ our Lord, Amen.
MISS LEAH.   Jesus wept!
SOPHIE.   Amen!
FANNIE.   Baker's a good man to take his wife back east to have her baby. I don't think she could have survived losing

another one out here.

MISS LEAH. These young women wouldn't have lasted a minute before the war. Overseer make you squat right down beside the field and drop your baby out like an animal. All ten of my sons was born after sundown 'cause that was the only way to be sure I could lay down to have 'em.

FANNIE. How did your babies know it was nighttime?

MISS LEAH. I knew it! If I felt 'em tryin' to come early, I'd hold 'em up in there and wouldn't let 'em. Bad enough bein' born a slave without that peckerwood overseer watchin' 'em take the first breath of life before their daddy done seen if they a boy or a girl child.

FANNIE. I think Miz Baker will be all right. I think she was just scared and lonesome for her mother. She can't be more than 20.

MISS LEAH. I wadn't but fourteen when I had my first one! Got up the next morning and strapped him on my back and went back out to the field. Overseer didn't notice him 'til the day half over. What you got there, nigger? He say to me. This here my son, I say. I callin' him Samson like in the bible 'cause he gonna be strong! Overseer laugh and say, good! Colonel Harrison always lookin' for strong niggers to pick his cotton. I want to tell him that not what I got in mind for my Samson, but I kept my mouth shut like I had some sense. I ain't never been no fool.

FANNIE. Wil said he didn't think there would be snow for another couple of weeks at least.

SOPHIE. If he's got that much time to chit chat maybe I can get him to help me repair that stretch of fence out beyond the north pasture.

FANNIE. He already did.

SOPHIE. He did? When?

FANNIE. Yesterday. He told me to tell you not to worry about it.

MISS LEAH. *(Enjoying Sophie's surprise.)* Now that Wil Parrish is a good man and a good neighbor. You can't ask for better than that. Don't you think so, Fan?

FANNIE. Yes. I do think so.

SOPHIE.   Are you sweet on Wil Parrish?

FANNIE.   We're friends, Sister.

MISS LEAH.   You could do a lot worse. And he likes you. I can tell it sure as you sittin' here. Look at her blush! We gonna have a weddin' come spring!

SOPHIE.   I already lost one sister. Don't give Fan away too!

MISS LEAH.   Shoot, you ought to be glad. Once Fan gets out of the way, you might find somebody fool enough to take a look at you.

SOPHIE.   Two things I'm sure of. I don't want no white folks tellin' me what to do all day, and no man tellin' me what to do all night.

MISS LEAH.   I'll say amen to that!

FANNIE.   *(Clearing up dishes.)* Do you want to work on your stories some tonight? *(Sophie takes out her shotgun and begins to clean and oil it. She breaks it down quickly and efficiently. She has done this a thousand times.)*

MISS LEAH.   I'm too tired.

FANNIE.   *(Coaxing.)* Let's just finish the one we were working on Sunday night.

MISS LEAH.   I keep tellin' you these ain't writin' stories. These are tellin' stories.

FANNIE.   Then tell them to me!

MISS LEAH.   So you can write 'em!

FANNIE.   So we can remember them.

MISS LEAH.   Colored folks can't forget the plantation any more than they can forget their own names. If we forget that, we ain't got no history past last week.

SOPHIE.   But you won't always be around to tell it.

MISS LEAH.   Long enough, Sister Sophie. Long enough. *(She gets up unsteadily.)* Good night, Fan.

FANNIE.   Good night, Miss Leah. *(Miss Leah looks at Sophie who speaks without looking up.)*

SOPHIE.   You're not going to be mad at me all winter, are you?

MISS LEAH.   Good night, Sister Sophie.

SOPHIE.   Good night, Miss Leah. *(Miss Leah exits.)*

FANNIE.   Why do you agitate her?

SOPHIE.   She'll live longer if she's doing it to irritate me. *(A beat.)* I need a new hoop for that back wheel and it won't be in by Friday. Do you think Wil Parrish has got plans for his wagon on Friday?

FANNIE.   You can ask him. He's going to stop by tomorrow ... to see Miss Leah.

SOPHIE.   Good ... I'm sure Miss Leah will be pleased to see him.

FANNIE.   I wish you wouldn't work at my desk. Look at this mess! What's this?

SOPHIE.   It's from Miss Lewiston.

FANNIE.   She's still coming isn't she? *(Anxiously reading the letter.)*

SOPHIE.   She "regrets she will be unable to fulfill the position of instructor at the Nicodemus School and wishes us the best of luck in finding someone else to assume this important responsibility."

FANNIE.   She's getting married.

SOPHIE.   And her husband's scared of life on the frontier. What kind of colored men are they raising in the city these days anyway?

FANNIE.   She didn't say he was scared.

SOPHIE.   She said he was nervous about moving to a place where there were still gangs of wild Indians at large.

FANNIE.   People are scared of different things.

SOPHIE.   No they're not. They're either scared or they're not.

FANNIE.   *(Folding up the letter; resigned to it.)* Do you ever regret it? Coming West like we did.

SOPHIE.   I never regret anything.

FANNIE.   I miss the conversation more than anything, I think.

SOPHIE.   Don't Miss Leah and I keep you amused?

FANNIE.   That wouldn't be the word I'd use. No! Of course you do. That's not what I mean ... I mean, the literary societies and the Sunday socials and the forums. Mama and Daddy's house was always full of people talking at the top of their lungs about the best way to save the race. And then somebody would start thumping away on Mama's old piano and begging her to sing something. I used to hide at the top of the steps and watch them until I'd fall asleep right there.

SOPHIE.   Well, Minnie ought to be able to fill you in on the latest in that kind of life.

FANNIE.   London, Sister. It may well be on another planet. I can't believe she'll really be here. It seems like she's been gone forever.

SOPHIE.   Almost a year and a half.

FANNIE.   Fifteen months, three weeks and five days.

SOPHIE.   But who's counting?

FANNIE.   I miss her so! If I try to talk her into staying longer, don't let me!

SOPHIE.   Why?

FANNIE.   You know how Frank feels about the frontier.

SOPHIE.   How can I stop you?

FANNIE.   Kick me under the table or something! At least she'll be here for her birthday. She said Frank thinks it will take a couple of weeks to get the will settled. I hope everything turns out all right. Frank is counting so much on this inheritance.

SOPHIE.   Frank better figure out how to work for a living! I picked up the new deeds today. One for you, one for me and one for Baby Sister. That ought to make her feel grown.

FANNIE.   She's not going to believe it.

SOPHIE.   Why? I always told her she'd have her share officially when she got old enough.

FANNIE.   Knowing you, I think she thought you meant about sixty-five! Sometimes I try to imagine what Baby Sister's life is like over there. How it feels. It must be exciting. Museums and theaters all over the place. She said Frank did a public recital from his book and there were fifty people there.

SOPHIE.   How many colored people were there?

FANNIE.   She didn't say.

SOPHIE.   None! No! Two! Her and Frank. Who ever heard of a colored poet moving someplace where there aren't any colored people?

FANNIE..   Where do you expect him to live? Nicodemus?

SOPHIE. Why not? I'm giving her the deed to one third of the land we're standing on and she's married to a man who'd rather take a tour of Piccadilly Circus!

FANNIE. Some people are not raised for this kind of life.

SOPHIE. Did we raise Min for the life she's living halfway around the world?

FANNIE. Of course, we did. We always exposed her to the finest things.

SOPHIE. But why do all those fine things have to be so far away from Negroes?

FANNIE. I think our baby sister is having so much fun out there in the world, coming back here is probably the last thing on her mind.

SOPHIE. Do you know how much land they could be buying with all that money they're running through living so high on the hog?

FANNIE. They've got plenty of time to buy land.

SOPHIE. All that money and the best he can think of to do with it is move to England and print up some books of bad poetry.

FANNIE. They weren't that bad.

SOPHIE. They were terrible! "Odes to Spring." You couldn't even tell a Negro wrote them.

FANNIE. What's so bad about that? We don't have to see spring differently just because we're Negroes, do we?

SOPHIE. We have to see everything differently because we're Negroes, Fan. I think Frank is going to find that out when they finish with this business about his father's will.

FANNIE. Min says Frank has hired a lawyer. You don't think they'll cut him out of the will, do you?

SOPHIE. How many white gentlemen do you know who want to share their inheritance with a bastard?

FANNIE. That's not fair.

SOPHIE. He's the one who kept talking about his father this and his father that and the man wouldn't even come to wedding!

FANNIE. Well, I just try to give him the benefit of the doubt. Mama said every colored man deserved at least that much from a colored woman.

SOPHIE.   Suit yourself. All I know is, we're going to have a school by spring if I have to teach in it myself!

FANNIE.   Poor children would be crazy before they had a chance to learn their ABCs!

SOPHIE.   *(Suddenly.)* Sh-h-h-h-h! *(She motions toward the candle and Fannie blows it out immediately. Sophie clicks the gun quickly into place and loads two shells into place. She goes quickly to the window and peers out. Fannie stands motionless, watching her. Sophie breathes a sigh of relief.)* Deer! Three of them! Come look. *(Sophie sets down the gun and the two stand looking at the deer in the moonlight.)* I'll be nice to Frank. For Min's sake. Butter won't melt in my mouth.

FANNIE.   Promise?

SOPHIE.   I promise. *(They embrace warmly. Fannie re-lights the candle and Sophie fixes the fire in the stove for the night.)* Did you talk Miss Leah out of going to the station with us?

FANNIE.   I think so.

SOPHIE.   You did? How?

FANNIE.   I told her you didn't think it was a good idea.

SOPHIE.   No wonder she's mad at me!

FANNIE.   She's always mad at you!

SOPHIE.   Well, good. Maybe she'll live to be a hundred! *(They exit for bed.)*

BLACKOUT

Scene 2

Sophie, Fannie and Wil are at the train station to meet Minnie and Frank. We hear the blast of the train whistle as the lights come up on the platform. Sophie and Wil are waiting patiently. Fannie is very excited.

FANNIE.   It's so hard to wait once you see it, isn't it? Why is it taking so long? It doesn't even look like it's moving very fast any more, does it?

SOPHIE. They're right on time.

WIL. And that's real lucky for you. This train don't never run on time.

FANNIE. But it's on time today, isn't it? And that's what counts!

WIL. Yes, it is, Miss Fannie. That's what counts!

FANNIE. Is it still moving? Can you tell? I can't tell! I'm going to find the station manager. *(She exits.)*

SOPHIE. Fan told me you took care of my fence.

WIL. Yes.

SOPHIE. That was very neighborly of you. I'm much obliged.

WIL. You're welcome.

SOPHIE. Would you like to have dinner with us this evening?

WIL. You don't have to ...

SOPHIE. I want you to come. And I'm sure Fan would enjoy having you.

WIL. Well, thank you. It'd be my ... *(Fannie enters, excitedly.)*

FANNIE. It's pulling in! Oh, Sophie, I'm so excited. Do you see them yet? Can you see them, Wil.

SOPHIE. I don't see any ... there she is!

FANNIE. Where? Where? I still don't ... Minnie! Min! Here! We're here! *(Minnie enters on the run. She is wearing a fur-trimmed coat and carrying a fur muff. Her hat dips fashionably low over her face.)*

MINNIE. Fannie! Oh, Fannie! *(They embrace.)* Oh, Sister! I missed you both so much!

FANNIE. Look at you in that outfit!

SOPHIE. How about that hat? Who are you hiding from?

MINNIE. *(Tugging it lower.)* They're all the rage in London!

SOPHIE. Where are your bags?

MINNIE. Frank has them. He stopped to send a telegram. He was talking to a man he met on the train ... a white man. Maybe I better ...

WIL. I'll give him a hand.

MINNIE. Thank you...?

FANNIE. Wil Parrish, meet my baby sister, Minnie.

WIL. Pleased to meet you.

MINNIE.   Pleased to be met. *(Wil exits.)*

FANNIE.   We borrowed Wil's wagon to pick you up.

SOPHIE.   And Wil came with it to make sure Miss Fannie got to town and back safely.

MINNIE.   Is he your sweetheart? Is he?

FANNIE.   Don't pay Sophie a bit of mind.

SOPHIE.   He's coming to dinner tonight. You can ask him yourself.

FANNIE.   You better not say a word! *(Frank has entered and stands watching them. Frank is immaculately dressed in fine clothes from head to toe. Coat, hat, suit, gloves, shirt — everything of the finest quality and very tasteful. The sheer richness of the clothing is obvious in every piece.)*

FRANK.   Secrets already?

MINNIE.   Darling! *(She runs to him and takes his arm protectively. Frank allows himself to be lead toward her sisters.)*

FANNIE.   *(Warmly.)* Frank. It's lovely to have you both! *(Frank puts down the small bag he's carrying and takes off one soft leather glove to extend his hand. Fannie kisses his cheek instead.)*

FRANK.   It's good to see you, too.

FANNIE.   I was so sorry to hear about your father.

FRANK.   Thank you.

FANNIE.   Well, I know it was a long trip, but you're here at last!

FRANK.   Nothing would do but Minnie had to come and see her sisters, isn't that right, darling?

FANNIE.   You don't mind sharing her with us once in awhile, do you?

FRANK.   Of course, not. And I've got some other things to share with you as well.

FANNIE.   *(Teasing and happy.)* Just how many riches do you think a poor frontier woman can stand at one time?

FRANK.   I thought you might enjoy having an autographed copy of Mr. Dunbar's latest volume. *(He hands her a small book of poetry.)*

FANNIE.   Autographed? I've been trying to get my hands on any copy for months!

MINNIE.   Frank walked me all over New Orleans to find it.

FANNIE.   How can I ever thank you?

FRANK.   It's my pleasure. *(A beat.)* Hello, Sophie.

SOPHIE.   *(Nods formally.)* Frank ...

FRANK.   We'll try not to overstay our welcome.

FANNIE.   Stay as long as you like. You're family.

MINNIE.   That's just what I told him. We're family! This isn't like coming for a visit. This is coming home.

FRANK.   But we have a home, don't we, darling?

MINNIE.   Yes, of course we do. We have a lovely home.

FANNIE.   And you're going to tell me all about ...

FRANK.   *(Interrupts her.)* And where is our home, Minnie?

MINNIE.   Frank ... *(He stares at her coldly.)* It's in London.

FRANK.   So this is really a visit, just like I said, isn't it?

MINNIE.   *(Softly.)* Yes, Frank.

FRANK.   *(False heartiness.)* Of course it is! And it's going to be a great visit. I'm sure of it. Well, how long does it take to get from here to there, anyway? I could do with a hot bath.

FANNIE.   Of course you could. Wil's probably got the wagon loaded. Come on! Come on! Miss Leah's at the house and I know she's pacing up and down at the window right now. *(Fannie hooks Minnie's arm and draws her away from Frank. Minnie looks back anxiously at Frank who stares at her impassively. He turns to find Sophie looking at him.)*

SOPHIE.   Welcome to Nicodemus, Frank. *(Frank tips his hat and bows slightly. He exits pulling on his gloves and leaving his small suitcase behind. Sophie looks after him, looks at the bag, shifts the shotgun easily to the crook of her arm, picks up the bag and exits.)*

BLACKOUT

Scene 3

Fannie is taking out plates, laying out food, etc. Miss Leah is tottering around impatiently, making it difficult for Fannie to accomplish her task without tripping over Miss Leah.

As we hear Miss Leah talking to Fannie, in the bedroom we see Minnie at the mirror trying to convince herself that her bruised face isn't that noticeable. Frank is taking off his jacket, unbuttoning his shirt, etc. He catches a glimpse of Minnie looking in the mirror. He goes to her, stands behind her. She puts her hand down. He turns her slowly to face him. He gently, tenderly touches her bruised face. She flinches. He kisses her gently. She relaxes and he kisses her more passionately. She breaks away playfully. She looks in the mirror with resignation, grabs up her hat and pulls it back on. One last look at Frank who still watches her. She throws him a kiss and goes out. He lays down on the bed, takes out a book and begins to read.

MISS LEAH.   I don't see why she has to help him get settled right this minute. He's a grown man. He can unpack a suitcase, can't he.

FANNIE.   I'm sure he can. I think Min just wants to make him feel at home here.

MISS LEAH.   Why wouldn't he feel at home here? *(Minnie enters quickly. She is nervous because she still wears her hat.)*

FANNIE.   Thank goodness. Miss Leah was about to send me back there to rescue you.

MINNIE.   Did you miss me?

MISS LEAH.   Lord, chile, I thought that man had tied you to the bed post back there. Take off that hat, honey, and let me look at you.

FANNIE.   Aren't the flowers wonderful? I've got all your favorites ... *(As Minnie slowly removes her hat, Fannie sees the large bruise above Minnie's left eye.)* Minnie! My god!

MINNIE.   *(Laughing nervously.)* It doesn't look that bad, does it?

MISS LEAH.   What happened to your face, chile?

MINNIE.   It's so silly. *(They wait in silence.)* I bought a new dress for the trip ... and I ... I wanted to show it to Frank ... and I ... the train ... I stumbled in the train compartment. You know how clumsy I am. I bumped my head so hard I saw stars! And this is what I've got to show for it. Frank made me promise to be more careful. He worries so about me. *(An awkward pause. They don't believe her.)* I told him I used to be much worse. Remember that time I almost fell off the roof I would have killed myself if it hadn't been for Sophie.

FANNIE.   Yes, I remember ...

MINNIE.   Don't look so worried. I'll be careful. It was just an accident.

FANNIE.   All right, Baby Sister. *(Sophie enters with wood in her arms.)*

MISS LEAH.   Close that door!

SOPHIE.   Let me get in it first. Your turn to chop tomorrow, Minnie. Being a world traveler doesn't excuse you from your chores! *(Sees the bruise on Minnie's face for the first time.)* What happened to your face?

MINNIE.   I took a tumble, that's all. It looks a lot worse than it is.

SOPHIE.   A tumble?

FANNIE.   Minnie was showing off for her handsome husband and lost her balance on the train.

MINNIE.   I know it looks awful. Here! I'll put my beautiful hat back on to hide it!

FANNIE.   No! Anything but that!

MINNIE.   Then let's not talk about it anymore. *(Sophie looks at Minnie and Fannie and takes off her coat, etc.)*

SOPHIE.   Suit yourself.

MISS LEAH.   How does living in ...

MINNIE.   London, Miss Leah. It's in England.

MISS LEAH.   How does it agree with you?

MINNIE.   Well, it was kind of scary to me at first. So many people and colored just right in there with everybody else.

MISS LEAH. No Jim Crow?

MINNIE. None.

MISS LEAH. I can't imagine such a thing.

MINNIE. That's why you have to come visit me. So you can see for yourself.

MISS LEAH. I don't need to see nothin' else new. I done seen enough new to last me. I don't know why anybody wants to be all up next to a bunch of strange white folks anyway.

SOPHIE. Because somebody told them they weren't supposed to!

MINNIE. Oh, they're not so bad. Frank and I even have some white ... friends.

MISS LEAH. Lord, deliver us! What is this chile talking about?

MINNIE. Frank says he doesn't see why he only has to be with Negroes since he has as much white blood in him as colored.

SOPHIE. Frank is talking crazy.

MINNIE. It's true. His father was ...

SOPHIE. A slaveowner! Just like mine.

MINNIE. Frank said his father wanted to marry his mother. They were ... in love.

SOPHIE. Did he free her?

MINNIE. No ...

SOPHIE. Then don't talk to me about love.

FANNIE. *(Quickly.)* Let's have some supper before you two start fighting. Min, go tell Frank to come to the table. *(Minnie exits to the bedroom as Wil approaches outside with flowers. Frank has gotten dressed up for dinner. When Minnie opens the door, he turns to her and strikes a pose for her approval. She kisses him and they go out arm in arm.)*

MISS LEAH. There's Wil Parrish at the door. *(Fannie opens the door as he raises his hand to knock.)*

FANNIE. You're just in time.

WIL. I stopped for ... these are for you.

FANNIE. They're lovely.

MISS LEAH. Just what we need.

WIL. Evenin', Miss Leah. How're you feelin'?

29

MISS LEAH.   I'd feel a whole lot better if people stopped lettin' that cold air in on me. *(Frank and Minnie enter arm in arm.)*

FRANK.   I'm starved!

FANNIE.   Good! Why don't you sit here next to Min? Wil, you sit here by ... Sophie. Miss Leah ...

WIL.   You're the first colored poet I ever saw.

FRANK.   How many white ones have you seen?

WIL..   None that I can recall ...

FRANK.   Then that makes me the first poet you've ever seen, doesn't it?

MINNIE.   Frank ... *(They settle into their places and join hands.)*

FANNIE.   Sister, will you bless the table?

SOPHIE.   Thank you for this food we are about to receive and for the safe journey of our beloved sister. *(A beat.)* And Frank. Amen.

ALL.   Amen. *(As they talk, the meal is served, consumed and cleared away.)*

FANNIE.   Did you have a good rest?

FRANK.   Enough to hold me, I guess. *(To Sophie.)* Min tells me you're a mulatto. *(Sophie is startled.)* Oh, excuse me! I didn't mean to be so personal. It's just that I'm a mulatto myself and I was interested to know if there are many of us this far west. You know you can't always tell by looking!

SOPHIE.   There are just a few.

FRANK.   I can understand why. This is a lot closer to the field then most of us ever want to get! *(Laughs.)*

MINNIE.   *(Quickly to Wil.)* This is my husband's first visit to the frontier.

WIL.   How do you like it so far?

FRANK.   So far, so good. But to tell the truth, I've always been more of a city person.

SOPHIE.   And what kind of person is that?

FRANK.   Oh, I think one who enjoys a little more ... ease than is possible way out here. Although I must admit your home is lovely. This table wouldn't be out of place in the finest dining rooms.

FANNIE.   Why thank you Frank!

SOPHIE.   Tomorrow we'll go back to eating around the campfire like we usually do.

MINNIE.   Don't listen to Sister! Fan is famous for setting the prettiest table in Nicodemus.

FRANK.   I admire the ability to adapt to trying circumstances without a lowering of standards. I wouldn't have expected to see such delicate china way out here.

FANNIE.   These were my mother's things. Sophie stopped speakin to me for a week when I told her I wasn't leaving Memphis without them, but I was determined.

SOPHIE.   I should have left you and them standing in the middle of Main Street. Whoever heard of carrying a set of plates ...

MINNIE.   Mama's china!

FANNIE.   Mama's good china!

SOPHIE.   A set of plates halfway across the country when we hardly had room for Min.

MINNIE.   You weren't going to leave me in the middle of Main Street, too, were you?

FANNIE.   She couldn't have left us. Who would she have had to boss around?

MINNIE.   I'd like to go back to Memphis sometime. Just to visit. Wouldn't you?

SOPHIE.   Not me! Colored folks lives aren't worth two cents in that town.

FANNIE.   But everybody says things have gotten a lot better.

FRANK.   Well, that may be true in Memphis, but we were in New Orleans to see my lawyers just before we came here and it's still pretty much the same as it's always been, if you ask me. They had just had a lynching the week before we got there. *(Laughs.)* Just my luck!

MINNIE.   After they hung the poor man they threw his body down in the street right in the middle of the colored section of town.

MISS LEAH.   Don't any of those New Orleans Negroes know how to use a shotgun?

FRANK.   He pretty much brought it on himself from what I heard down at the bank. He was involved in some ...

31

SOPHIE. *(Cuts him off.)* I don't care what he was involved in.

FRANK. Doesn't it matter?

SOPHIE. No. Whatever it was, he didn't deserve to die like that.

FRANK. Well, I stand corrected. And I do apologize for introducing such inappropriate dinner table conversation.

MISS LEAH. I don't know why those Negroes stay down there!

SOPHIE. Because they haven't got the gumption to try something new. The day our group left Memphis, there were at least two hundred other Negroes standing around, rolling their eyes and trying to tell us we didn't know what it was going to be like way out here in the wilderness. I kept trying to tell them it doesn't matter what it's like. Any place is better than here!

FRANK. Well, that's something we agree on!

WIL. I'll say "amen" to that, too! If I never set foot in the Confederacy again, it's too soon for me.

FANNIE. Oh, no! You two can't start thinking like Sister! One Sophie is enough.

MISS LEAH. Too many if you ask me.

MINNIE. Has her coffee gotten any better?

MISS LEAH. Worse! And her disposition neither. I don't know how I'm gonna make it through the winter with her.

MINNIE. She's not so bad. You just have to remember to put cotton in your ears.

FRANK. I wish I'd thought of that on the train. Min was so excited she was talking a mile a minute the whole way out here. Weren't you, darling? She hardly took a deep breath.

MINNIE. I wasn't that bad, was I?

FRANK. I didn't want to hurt your feelings, darling, but you must have told me the same stories ten times!

MINNIE. I didn't mean to ...

SOPHIE. *(Cuts her off.)* Which one was your favorite?

FRANK. Oh, I think probably the one about you coming to the door asking to do the laundry and then moving right in. I guess you knew a good thing when you saw one!

MINNIE. Frank!

FRANK. What is it, darling? That is the way the story goes, isn't it?

FANNIE. I don't know what a good thing we were. Mama and Daddy both gone with the fever. So many people dying there weren't enough left well to take care of the sick ones. I was only twelve and Min still a baby.

MINNIE. So when Sophie came asking about doing the laundry, Fan asked her when she could start and Sophie said I can start right now. I'm free as a bird! And once she came, it was like she'd always been there.

FANNIE. I loved the way she said it. I was scared to death and here was this one talking about free as a bird.

WIL. Are you gonna put that in the book?

MINNIE. What book?

FANNIE. I'm writing a book about Nicodemus. I'm going to call it *The True History and Life Stories of Nicodemus, Kansas: A Negro Town.*

MINNIE. That sounds wonderful. Now we'll have two writers in the family.

FANNIE. Oh, I'm not really a writer. I'm more of a collector.

MINNIE. You could have a whole book with just Miss Leah's stories!

FANNIE. Well, some people don't think their stories are important enough to put in a book.

MISS LEAH. I'm not studyin' you, Fannie May Dove.

MINNIE. Why? I don't remember a time we went to your house when I didn't come back with a story.

MISS LEAH. Everybody knows them stories I got. Colored folks ain't been free long enough to have forgot what it's like to be a slave.

MINNIE. But you didn't always talk about slavery. You talked about how blue the sky would be in the summertime and about how you and the other children would sneak off from prayer meeting to play because you didn't want to work all week and pray all Sunday.

MISS LEAH. And got beat for it just as regular as a clock.

MINNIE.   You used to tell me about how all your babies had such fat little legs, remember?

MISS LEAH.   And where are they now? All them babies. All them grandbabies? Gone! Every last one of 'em!

MINNIE.   But you loved them, Miss Leah. Who's going to know how much you loved them?

FRANK.   Min's got a story, don't you darling?

MINNIE.   I thought you'd heard enough of my stories on the train.

FRANK.   But you haven't told our story, darling.

MINNIE.   I don't think this is ...

FANNIE.   Please? It's such a lovely story. With a happy ending.

FRANK.   Go ahead, now. Don't be silly.

MINNIE.   I was at school ...

FANNIE.   The conservatory ... go on!

MINNIE.   It was ... it was spring. The campus was lovely then. Flowers were everywhere. But all anybody kept talking about was the handsome stranger who was here visiting for a couple of weeks.

FANNIE.   That was Frank, all the way from England!

SOPHIE.   Fannie! Let her tell it, or you tell it!

FANNIE.   Go on! Sorry!

MINNIE.   Pretty soon, everybody but me had met him or at least seen him. And then one afternoon, I was out walking and I thought I was alone, so I started singing and Frank was out walking too and he heard me.

FRANK.   I really scared her!

MINNIE.   I hadn't heard him behind me.

FRANK.   I was tracking her like a wild Indian! *(Wil looks up sharply, but lets it pass.)*

MINNIE.   And then he said ...

FRANK.   I had been away from England for almost a month and I hadn't heard a note of Puccini in all that time. So I told her she sang like an angel and invited her to have dinner with me.

MINNIE.   And I said my sisters hadn't raised me to have dinner with a strange gentleman who I met on a walk in the woods.

SOPHIE.   You shouldn't have been walking in the woods alone in the first place.

FANNIE.   But then it wouldn't be a love story! Go on, Min.

MINNIE.   So I walked away and left him standing there.

FANNIE.   And the next day a friend of hers invited her to attend an evening of Negro poetry at the Chitauqua Literary Society ...

MINNIE.   And I looked behind the podium and there was Frank!

FRANK.   I recognized her right away ...

MINNIE.   And he nodded to me like we were old friends.

FANNIE.   And then he dedicated a poem to her.

MINNIE.   "A Song" by Mr. Paul Laurence Dunbar.

FRANK.
"Thou art the soul of a summer's day,
Thou art the breath of the rose.
But the summer is fled
And the rose is dead.
Where are they gone, who knows, who knows?"

MISS LEAH.   A Negro wrote that?

FANNIE.   And me and Sister dashed down to New Orleans in time enough for the wedding and to see them set sail back to England.

FRANK.   We'd only known each other a few weeks, but I knew Minnie was the girl for me. And she still is. *(He kisses her gently and she blushes.)*

FANNIE.   Beautiful! Now you tell one, Sister!

SOPHIE.   I don't want to bore Frank with stories he's heard before.

MINNIE.   Tell about the ritual. Tell about the day we left Memphis and came west to be free women.

SOPHIE.   Fan's the one always thinking up ceremonies. Let her tell it.

FANNIE.   Not this one! This came straight from you!

SOPHIE.   When we got ready to leave Memphis ...

MINNIE.   When you two got ready. I was too little to get a vote.

35

SOPHIE. Well, I knew it was the right thing to do. Memphis was full of crazy white men acting like when it came to colored people, they didn't have to be bound by law or common decency. Dragging people off in the middle of the night. Doing whatever they felt like doing. Colored women not safe in their own houses. Then I heard there were Negroes going west.

MISS LEAH. Been done gone!

SOPHIE. Then that crazy Pap Singleton came to the church looking for people to sign up to go to Kansas. That man had eyes like hot coals. He said he was like Moses leading the children of Israel out of bondage in Egypt.

FANNIE. Sister didn't even let the man finish talking before she ran down the aisle to sign up! I think Reverend Thomas thought she had finally gotten the spirit!

SOPHIE. Pap said there'd be all-colored towns, full of colored people only! That sounded more like heaven then anything else I'd heard in church.

MINNIE. Why does that make you smile?

WIL. That's what landed me in Nicodemus, too. Looking for some neighbors that looked like me.

FRANK. At home, we go for weeks and never see another colored face. A few Indians once in awhile — the Eastern kind — but that's not really the same thing is it?

MISS LEAH. Don't you get lonesome for colored people?

FRANK. To tell you the truth, I've seen about all the Negroes I need to see in this life. *(Laughs.)*

MINNIE. *(Quickly.)* Finish about the ritual, Sister!

SOPHIE. Another time.

MINNIE. Please!

FRANK. Don't whine, darling. Maybe Sophie is tired of talking.

MISS LEAH. Well, if she is, or if she ain't, I'm tired of listenin'!

MINNIE. You're not leaving us already, are you?

MISS LEAH. Knowing how long-winded some of the people at this table can be you all will probably be sittin' here when I get up tomorrow mornin'. *(She gets up unsteadily.)*

36

MINNIE.   Let me help you.

MISS LEAH.   One thing a woman my age should have the good sense to do alone is go to bed. Good night.

MINNIE, WIL, FANNIE, and SOPHIE.   Good night, Miss Leah. *(Fannie and Minnie begin clearing off the dishes. Wil unobtrusively helps them. Frank pours himself another glass of wine.)*

FRANK.   They don't make you do the woman's work around here too, do they Parrish?

WIL.   Makes it go quicker when everybody does a part.

FANNIE.   I couldn't have said it better myself! *(Sophie puts on her coat.)*

MINNIE.   Where are you off to?

SOPHIE.   To bring in a little more of that wood I spent all week chopping in your honor.

MINNIE.   Then the least I can do is help you carry it!

FANNIE.   I'll help, too! *(They throw on their shawls and almost rush out the door.)*

FRANK.   You know the night air doesn't agree with you, Minnie!

FANNIE.   We'll keep her warm, I promise. *(Pulls shawl over Min's head and pulls her out the door. Moonlight illuminates the yard. Wood is cut in a stack near the house.)*

SOPHIE.   What's he talking about? You're healthy as a horse.

MINNIE.   He just worries about me sometimes, that's all. I haven't been so strong lately ...

FANNIE.   But you're home now. I've got a whole week to toughen you up again!

MINNIE.   I'm counting on it. *(A beat.)* Sister?

SOPHIE.   Yes?

MINNIE.   Don't mind what Frank said about you coming to the door looking to do the laundry.

SOPHIE.   Didn't I come to your door?

MINNIE.   Yes ...

SOPHIE.   And didn't you need somebody to do the laundry?

MINNIE.   Yes, but, sometimes Frank says things in a way that ... that doesn't sound like how I know he means them.

SOPHIE.   I'm not ashamed of anything I've ever done and

if I was, taking in laundry to make an honest living wouldn't be the thing I'd pick. *(A beat.)* You don't have to apologize to me for your husband Min. If he's good to you, he's good enough for me. Is he good to you, Min?

MINNIE.   Yes, he's good to me.

SOPHIE.   Then he's all right with me.

FANNIE.   Well, since you two are getting along so well, let's do it before you start fussing again!

MINNIE.   Do what?

FANNIE.   The ritual. Let's do it now!

MINNIE.   Oh, yes, please! Can we? *(Wil can be seen sharpening a small knife on a stone. Frank takes out a cigar, prepares it, smokes. The women stand in a circle, holding hands.)*

SOPHIE.   Because we are free Negro women ...

FANNIE and MINNIE.   Because we are free Negro women ...

SOPHIE.   Born of free Negro women ...

FANNIE and MINNIE.   Born of free Negro women ...

ALL.   Back as far as time begins ...

SOPHIE.   We choose this day to leave a place where our lives, our honor and our very souls are not our own.

FANNIE.   Say it, Sister!

SOPHIE.   We choose this day to declare our lives to be our own and no one else's. And we promise to always remember the day we left Memphis and went west together to be free women as a sacred bond between us with all our trust.

FANNIE and MINNIE.   With all our trust ...

SOPHIE.   And all our strength ...

FANNIE and MINNIE.   And all our strength ... *(As they talk, Frank walks over to the window, smoking. He looks at the women holding hands in the moonlight.)*

SOPHIE.   And all our courage ...

FANNIE and MINNIE.   And all our courage ...

SOPHIE.   And all our love.

FANNIE and MINNIE.   And all our love. *(A beat.)*

SOPHIE.   Welcome home, Baby Sister. *(The three embrace, laughing happily. Frank still watches from the window.)*

BLACKOUT

Scene 4

Miss Leah is on the stage alone. She is mending something. Minnie kisses the sleeping Frank in the bedroom and goes quietly out, closing the door behind her. She is brushing her hair. She looks much younger than she did with her fancy hat and sophisticated hairdo.

MINNIE.   You're up early.

MISS LEAH.   Habit, chile. I don't know how to sleep past sun up.

MINNIE.   Where are Fan and Sister?

MISS LEAH.   Fan's already up washing and Sophie's probably off somewhere driving some other poor soul crazy. Come sit by me, chile. I couldn't hardly get a word in at dinner last night.

MINNIE.   You always hold your own.

MISS LEAH.   If you don't hold it, who gone hold it? Let me look at you. *(A beat.)* You look more like yourself this morning.

MINNIE.   I'm going to braid my hair with ribbons like you used to do it, remember?

MISS LEAH.   I remember. *(Minnie messes up a braid.)* But don't look like you do. Sit down here, girl, and let me fix that head. *(Minnie sits with her head between Miss Leah's knees.)*

MINNIE.   Don't you think Frank is fine looking?

MISS LEAH.   He'll do.

MINNIE.   I want all my babies to look just like him!

MISS LEAH.   He ain't that pretty.

MINNIE.   Do you think I'll be a good mother?

MISS LEAH.   You better be. Fan gone be too old for many babies by the time her and Wil stop dancin' around each other and Sophie's too mean for anybody to marry. So I'm countin' on you, Baby Sister. None of this makes any sense without the children.

MINNIE.   It would be hard to have a child way out here.

MISS LEAH.   There's a lot worse places than this to have a baby. I'd of given anything to a had my babies in my own little house on my own piece of land with James pacing outside and the midwife knowin' what to do to ease you through it. Is that too tight?

MINNIE.   It's perfect! *(Frank gets up and begins dressing in the bedroom. He is wearing more expensive city clothes. He takes great care with his cuff links, tie, etc. He is especially pleased with his hair.)*

MISS LEAH.   *(Resumes her braiding.)* I was only thirteen when I got my first one. They wanted me to start early 'cause I was big and strong. Soon as my womanhood came on me, they took me out in the barn and put James on me. He was older than me and big. He already had children by half the women on the place. My James ... *(A beat.)* But that first time, he was hurting me so bad and I was screamin' and carryin' on somethin' awful and that old overseer just watchin' and laughin' to make sure James really doin' it. He watch us every night for a week and after the third one I hear James tryin' to whisper somethin' to me real quiet while he doin' it. I was so surprised I stopped cryin' for a minute and I hear James sayin' "Leah, Leah, Leah...." He just kept sayin' my name over and over. *(A beat.)* At the end of the week, I had got my first son. Do you have another ribbon? *(Minnie hands her one from her pocket.)* Fan's gonna skin you about her ribbons, Missy!

MINNIE.   Did you love James?

MISS LEAH.   I always thought I would've if they'd a let me find him for myself. The way it was, we stayed together after the war 'cause we was closer to each other than to anybody that wadn't dead or sold off and because James said we had ten babies that they sold away from us. We ought to have ten more we could raise free. Done! *(Finishes the braiding.)*

MINNIE.   I love my hair in braids.

MISS LEAH.   Braid it or shave it off, I say. All the rest takes too much fussin' with. Don't leave a woman no time to think.

MINNIE.   Why won't you let Fannie write down your stories?

MISS LEAH.   Everything can't be wrote down. No matter

what Fannie tell you, some things gotta be said out loud to keep the life in 'em.

MINNIE.   Do you think James would have liked Kansas?

MISS LEAH.   I think he would of if he could have walked his mind this far from Tennessee. It takes some doin' to be able to see a place in your mind where you never been before.

MINNIE.   Frank's been so many places. London. Paris. Rome. Sometimes it seems like he's been everywhere and seen everything.

MISS LEAH.   Well, I know that ain't true.

MINNIE.   Why?

MISS LEAH.   'Cause this is his first time in Nicodemus.

MINNIE.   I kept hoping he would like it here. I miss it so much. I tried to describe it to him, and sometimes I'd read him Fannie's letters, but ...

MISS LEAH.   Well, some people truly are city people. They like all that noise and confusion. It gives them somethin' to hide behind. Can't do that out here. First winter teach you that. Out here, nothin' stands between you and your soul.

MINNIE.   It's more than that for Frank. He doesn't just hate the South and the frontier. He hates the whole country.

MISS LEAH.   Well, maybe the boy's got more sense then I thought he did.

MINNIE.   He said the first time he went to Europe he begged his father to leave him behind when it was time to go back to New Orleans. But he was only fourteen so his father refused.

MISS LEAH.   Fourteen can be a grown man if you let it.

MINNIE.   But he said he knew right then that as soon as he could, he was going to get on a boat for England and never look back. And he did, too.

MISS LEAH.   *(A beat.)* Baby?

MINNIE.   Yes?

MISS LEAH.   Do you ever miss colored people?

MINNIE.   I miss colored people so much sometime I don't know what to do!

MISS LEAH.   Well, that's good to hear. I thought you might

be getting as tired of Negroes as Frank seems to be.

MINNIE.   Frank doesn't mean any harm. He just doesn't feel like we do about Negroes. He might miss a friend or two, but when I ask him if he doesn't ever just miss being in a big group of Negroes, knowing that we are all going to laugh at the same time and cry at the same time just because we're all there being colored, he just shakes his head. I don't think he's ever felt it, so he can't miss it.

MISS LEAH.   How can a Negro get that grown and not know how it feels to be around his own people.

MINNIE.   He isn't used to being treated like other colored people. He gets so angry when we have to get on the Jim Crow car. When we can't go in the restaurants. I think if Frank had to live here, he might go mad.

MISS LEAH.   Well, Negroes are supposed to get mad, so that's a good sign.

MINNIE.   Not get mad, Miss Leah. Go mad.

MISS LEAH.   Six of one. Half a dozen of the other. *(Frank enters from the bedroom.)*

FRANK.   Good morning! Darling! I didn't hear you get up.

MINNIE.   *(Jumps up to hug him quickly.)* I didn't want to wake you.

FRANK.   What have you done to your hair?

MINNIE.   Miss Leah braided it for me like she used to? Do you like it?

FRANK.   I've never seen you with your hair in plaits.

MINNIE.   Yes you have. I was wearing braids when you met me.

FRANK.   *(Being charming for the benefit of Miss Leah.)* You looked like such a little country girl then. When I first took Minnie to London, I made sure to take her shopping before I introduced her to my friends. But I always knew she had potential. Anybody could see that. And that's why I married her. Because Minnie deserves the best. Doesn't she?

MISS LEAH.   She is the best.

FRANK.   Yes, she is! I'm going to step out for a smoke, if you two will excuse me.

MINNIE.   I'll come, too. Do you want me to make you some

breakfast before we go out? My coffee isn't as bad as Sister's.

MISS LEAH. Fan left me a fresh pot. Go ahead, chile. I'll be fine. I've been up long enough to be lookin' for a nap soon. *(Frank and Minnie exit to the yard.)*

FRANK. *(Angrily.)* I want you to put your hair back the way it was.

MINNIE. I always wore my ...

FRANK. You look like a damn picaninny! We haven't been here twenty-four hours and look at you.

MINNIE. I'm sorry ...

FRANK. You're always sorry, aren't you? Of course you are, but if you weren't so busy being sorry, you'd know there are some interesting things going on in Nicodemus these days.

MINNIE. What do you mean?

FRANK. Nothing. I'm going to ride into town to check at the telegraph office and ... take a look around.

MINNIE. Don't be too late, will you? *(He exits. Minnie sits down on the porch wearily and draws her knees to her chest, rocking back and forth wearily. In the kitchen, Fannie and Sophie are oblivious.)*

BLACKOUT

Scene 5

It is late that evening. Sophie and Fannie and Minnie are up. Fannie is sewing something. Sophie is pulling some papers from her desk. Some of these are rolled maps or plans, etc. These are Sophie's plans for the development of the town. Minnie is standing at the window. Fannie takes off her glasses, rubs her eyes sleepily. Minnie goes over to the fire and stirs it up, puts another log on.

FANNIE. Well, I think I'm going to leave the rest to you night owls! Don't worry. Nicodemus isn't big enough for Frank to get into trouble, even if he's looking for it.

MINNIE.   Good night.

FANNIE.   I'll be up early.

MINNIE.   Me, too. *(They embrace. Fannie takes her sewing and exits, patting Sophie affectionately as she passes.)*

FANNIE.   Good night, Sister.

SOPHIE.   Check on Miss Leah?

FANNIE.   Always. *(She exits. Sophie pours herself a cup of coffee.)*

MINNIE.   You don't have to wait up with me.

SOPHIE.   I won't be sleeping much between now and the vote next week.

MINNIE.   What are you doing?

SOPHIE.   I'm writing my speech for Sunday. I'm going to single-handedly convince these Negroes they have the right to protect their land from speculators and save Nicodemus!

MINNIE.   Save it from what?

SOPHIE.   From being just one more place where colored people couldn't figure out how to be free.

MINNIE.   Are politics so important?

SOPHIE.   *(A beat.)* Come look at this. *(Sophie has spread out the plans on the table.)* These are the plans for Nicodemus. Here's the store and the post office. In the same places, but bigger. And open every day, not just two days a week. And here's the blacksmith and the school ...

MINNIE.   Who did this?

SOPHIE.   I did. We want the school open by spring but the teacher we hired just wrote to say she won't come because she's getting married and her fool husband ... *(Sophie stops herself abruptly, not wanting to seem critical of Frank.)*

MINNIE.   Doesn't like the frontier, huh?

SOPHIE.   I guess not.

MINNIE.   This is wonderful.

SOPHIE.   Fan drew the buildings. I was just going to write down what was going where, but Fan said, how about all the people in Nicodemus who can't read? *(A beat.)* So the school goes here. The church stays where it is, but bigger. We've got fifty now in the Baptist pews alone! Then the doctor and the dentist will be here together so folks won't have to get their nerve up but once to go inside since it's different offices, but the same building. And see right here?

MINNIE. Yes.

SOPHIE. That's Fan's newspaper office and book publishing company.

MINNIE. Look! She put a little face waving out the window!

SOPHIE. That's her. Fan put us all on it. Here I am at the feed store. And here's Wil at the blacksmith. Here you are at the train station. Miss Leah's on here some place ...

MINNIE. She forgot to draw Frank.

SOPHIE. I guess she did.

MINNIE. You know I'd come back if I could, don't you?

SOPHIE. I think you would if you wanted to.

MINNIE. It's not that simple.

SOPHIE. Why isn't it?

MINNIE. Does anybody really know what they want? Do you?

SOPHIE. Of course I do! I want this town to be a place where a colored woman can be free to live her life like a human being. I want this town to be a place where a colored man can work as hard for himself as we used to work for white folks. I want a town where a colored child can go to anybody's door and be treated like they belong there.

MINNIE. When you start talking about this place, you make it sound like paradise for colored people.

SOPHIE. It's not paradise yet, but it can be beautiful. The century is going to change in two years. This can be a great time for colored people. We can really be free instead of spending our lives working for the same people that used to own us. How are we ever going to be free if we have to spend all of our time doing somebody else's laundry?

MINNIE. You used to do laundry.

SOPHIE. There's nothing wrong with doing laundry until you start thinking that's all you can do. That's why the vote is so important. We have to help each other stay strong. The rule doesn't say they can't sell their land. It says they can't sell it unless they are prepared to look the rest of us in the eye and say who they are selling it to and why. As long as they have to face each other, nobody will have nerve enough to sell to speculators, no matter what they're offering.

MINNIE.   But it wouldn't matter as long as most of the people here are colored, would it?

SOPHIE.   If we start selling to speculators everything will change. We may as well move back to Memphis. And before I do that, I'll get Wil Parrish to teach me how to speak Spanish and move us all to Mexico! *(She starts gathering up her maps, etc.)*

MINNIE.   Wait, before you put it away. I was thinking maybe you could show it to Frank. So he could see how nice everything is going to be.

SOPHIE.   Mr. Frank Charles ain't no more interested in an all-colored town than the man in the moon.

MINNIE.   Frank's not so bad, Sister.

SOPHIE.   Suit yourself.

MINNIE.   Why don't you like him?

SOPHIE.   I don't have to like him.

MINNIE.   I know. But why don't you?

SOPHIE.   I think Frank hates being colored. I don't understand Negroes like that. They make me nervous.

MINNIE.   *(Stung.)* You make me nervous.

SOPHIE.   I didn't used to.

MINNIE.   No. I guess you didn't. *(Sophie picks up the gun, puts on her coat.)*

SOPHIE.   I'm going to check the horses. *(She exits. Minnie goes over to stoke the fire, hears a noise. Frank crosses the yard quickly and enters. Minnie turns, thinking it is Sophie. She freezes.)*

FRANK.   What are you still doing up? It's late. *(He staggers over, sits and drinks a long pull from a silver flask without taking his eyes off of her.)*

MINNIE.   I was waiting for you.

FRANK.   Why? Haven't I had enough bad luck for a nigger?

MINNIE.   Are you all right?

FRANK.   Do I look like I'm all right?

MINNIE.   Let me get you some coffee ...

FRANK.   You don't need to get me a damn thing. Just sit still! Can you just sit still for once.

MINNIE.   Yes, Frank.

FRANK.   You know what happened tonight, don't you? I don't even have to bother telling you anything about it, do I?

MINNIE. What is it? What happened?

FRANK. I was gambling. A gentleman's game of poker with some of my friends from the train. Ran into them in town. And you know what? I lost. I lost everything. What there was left of it.

MINNIE. You were gambling with white men?

FRANK. White gentlemen, Min. And I lost every dime. And I want to thank you for that. Things were going fine until one of them asked me about the nigger woman who kept following me around the train. I laughed it off, but my luck changed after that so I know they suspected something. *(He stands behind her, touching her shoulders lightly.)* But I should have known better then to depend on you for luck. You're too black to bring me any good luck. All you got to give is misery. Pure D misery and little black pickaninnies just like you. *(He rubs her arms, stops, keeping his hands lightly on her shoulders. She moves away in fear.)*

MINNIE. Frank, were you ...

FRANK. Shut up! *(She looks around for help in a panic.)* But the game wasn't a total loss. I found out something interesting. Do you know what I found out?

MINNIE. No Frank.

FRANK. Your sisters are sitting on a fortune. That white man on the train? He said speculators are paying top dollar for these farms around here.

MINNIE. Sister would never sell this land!

FRANK. Of course she wouldn't because she's just like all the other Negroes around here. She's content to live her life like a pack mule out in some backwater town.... I never should have let you talk me into bringing you out here. We damn well could have waited in New Orleans like I wanted to. Taking that damn train all the way across the damn prairie. You know what they call your precious town? "Niggerdemus"! Niggerdemus, Kansas. Don't you think that's funny, Min?

MINNIE. Were you passing?

FRANK. I was letting people draw their own conclusions.

MINNIE. Who did you tell them I was?

FRANK. I told you to shut up! *(He pushes her roughly and she stumbles and falls to the floor at the moment that Sophie enters from the porch. Fannie follows almost immediately, awakened by the noise.)*

FANNIE. Minnie! My God!

SOPHIE. What do you think you're doing?

FRANK. I'm talking to my wife. This is none of your affair.

MINNIE. It's all right! It was an accident. I just slipped, didn't I, Frank? I just slipped.

SOPHIE. Get out.

FRANK. You're pretty high and mighty for a nigger woman, aren't you?

MINNIE. Shut up, Frank! He's drunk! Don't listen to him!

FRANK. What did you say? *(He starts to move toward Minnie in a threatening manner. Sophie raises the shotgun and cocks it.)*

MINNIE. No, Sister! Don't! Please don't! I'm going to have a baby! *(All stop.)*

BLACKOUT

END OF ACT ONE

ACT TWO

Scene 1

It is early the next morning. Sophie is standing at the window with her gun at her side. Frank is skulking around in the yard, coatless and cold. Fannie is getting a tea kettle off the stove. Miss Leah is taking some herbs from small jars laid out before her and preparing them for the tea. Minnie is wrapped in a blanket, propped up in a chair. She looks fragile and frightened.

MINNIE. He doesn't even have his coat with him.

SOPHIE. Good! Maybe he'll freeze to death.

FANNIE. Don't say that. You'll just upset her again.

SOPHIE. Upset her? Don't you think she ought to be upset? Don't you think we all ought to be upset?

MISS LEAH. Let her drink this tea and catch her breath before you start fussin' again. *(Frank exits the yard. Miss Leah ands cup to Min.)* Drink all of it. It'll help you hold onto that baby.

MINNIE. This is such a hard time for Frank ...

SOPHIE. For Frank?

MINNIE. He's my husband!

FANNIE. Of course he is. Be still, now.

MINNIE. He's so afraid they will try to trick him out of his inheritance.

SOPHIE. Of course they will! ˎ

FANNIE. Sister, please!

MINNIE. His brothers hate him.

SOPHIE. His brothers used to own him!

MINNIE. That's not his fault too, is it?

SOPHIE. No. It's his fault for thinking that means they owe him something and if he doesn't get it, he has the right to put his hands on you.

49

MINNIE. I love him.

SOPHIE. That's not love.

MINNIE. *(A beat.)* How would you know? *(Sophie looks at Minnie, picks up the shotgun and goes to sit on the porch steps. Miss Leah looks at Minnie then goes to get a pipe and prepares it slowly.)*

FANNIE. You know, Sister only wants what is best for you.

MINNIE. I know.

FANNIE. Sometimes I think if I'd known you were going to stay so long, I'd of thought longer about letting you go.

MINNIE. Me too. *(A beat.)* Everything has changed. Everything. When Frank and I went to London, it was like a fairy tale. I felt so free! I could do anything, go anywhere, buy anything. And Frank was always there to show me something I had never seen before or tell me something I'd been waiting to hear all my life ... and I loved to look at him. But then he changed.... He was mad all the time.

FANNIE. Mad at who?

MINNIE. At everybody. But mostly me, I guess.

MISS LEAH. Why was he mad at you?

MINNIE. I don't know why! I think he just started hating colored people. We'd be walking down the street and he'd say: "Look at those niggers. No wonder nobody wants to be around them." When his father died and his brothers stopped sending money, it just got worse and worse. It was almost like he couldn't stand to look at me ...

FANNIE. Hush, now. It's all right. Me and Miss Leah will take care of you now. There's not a baby in the world that can come before Miss Leah says it's time to.

MINNIE. Sometimes I used to think it must be a dream and that I'd wake up one day and Frank would be the way he used to be.

MISS LEAH. Grown people don't change except to get more like what they already are.

FANNIE. Frank is going through a bad time that's all but he's still Frank. He's still that man that swept you off your feet. The man you want to be the father of your children, isn't he?

MINNIE. He scares me sometimes. He gets so angry.

FANNIE. You know who else had a terrible temper?

MINNIE.   Who?

FANNIE.   Daddy. You were too young to remember it, but he did. And Daddy was a good man, but he had that temper and sometimes it would get the better of him. Just like your Frank. Sometimes he used to ... not all the time, but ... one time they woke me up, fussing about something, and Mama didn't hear me call her, so I went to the top of the stairs where I could see them without them seeing me. I always sat there ... Daddy was sitting by the fireplace and Mama was talking a mile a minute. I could tell he didn't like what she was saying, and then he got up real fast and grabbed her arm and he just shook her and shook her ... I was so scared I ran back to bed, but I could still hear everything.... Sometimes we have to be stronger then they are, Baby Sister. We have to understand and be patient.

MINNIE.   What did Mama do?

FANNIE.   Mama always said she was biding her time until we could get these white folks of our backs so she could get colored men straightened out on a thing or two a little bit closer to home, but until then, she said she'd give him the benefit of the doubt.

MINNIE.   I've been trying to do that, too.

FANNIE.   You love Frank, don't you?

MINNIE.   I used to love him so much ...

FANNIE.   You still love him. I can see it on your face. You two can work it out. I know you can. For better or for worse, remember?

MINNIE.   I'll try. I'll really try. *(Frank enters the yard and Minnie sees him from the window.)* Frank! *(She rushes past Sophie on the porch and into his arms. He embraces her and grins evilly at Sophie.)*

BLACKOUT

Scene 2

Fannie and Miss Leah are up and ready for church. Sophie is finishing breakfast at the table alone. Frank and Minnie are in their room getting ready to go.

FANNIE.   How was everything?

SOPHIE.   Fine. Thank you.

FANNIE.   Is your speech ready?

SOPHIE.   As ready as it's going to be. I'm not going to worry about it. I'll say what I have to say and then we'll see which way it goes.

FANNIE.   It'll go your way. You've hardly been home at all this week, out convincing everybody.

MISS LEAH.   That's not why she hasn't been around here this week. Is it?

SOPHIE.   I don't know what you mean. *(Sophie clears up her plate while Miss Leah watches her.)*

MISS LEAH.   You are the most stubborn colored woman I've ever seen in my life.

SOPHIE.   I'll take that as a compliment coming from you.

FANNIE.   Please don't get her started! I want us to ride to church and back in peace.

SOPHIE.   I can't tell her who to marry, but I won't sit at a table with a man who called me an uppity nigger woman in my own damn house!

FANNIE.   She's forgiven him. Can't you?

SOPHIE.   He doesn't want my forgiveness. And she doesn't need it. She hasn't done anything wrong.

FANNIE.   He made a mistake. He's sorry. I know he is. You haven't spoken a word to either one of them in a week. London is so far away and she'll be gone soon. Don't let her go without a word.

MISS LEAH.   Colored women ain't got enough sisters to be cutting each other off so easy, I'd say.

SOPHIE.   I pointed a gun at the man's head and wanted to use it!

FANNIE.   And he's prepared to sit at table with you!

MISS LEAH.   Which shows he ain't as smart as he thinks he is! *(Suddenly, Sophie laughs.)*

SOPHIE.   All right, you win!

FANNIE.   Thank goodness! Now we can celebrate this birthday right!

SOPHIE.   Don't get carried away. I said I'd be here. I didn't say I'd talk.

FANNIE.   You know how special this birthday is. For all of us. How can you give her the deed if you won't even talk to her?

SOPHIE.   You give it to her. *(Puts the envelope with the deed in front of Fannie.)*

FANNIE.   I can't. Not without you. It has to be all three of us or it doesn't mean anything. "With all our trust. And all our strength. And all our courage. And all our love." Remember? *(Minnie and Frank enter from the back, ready for church. They both stop when they see Sophie is still there.)*

MINNIE.   Good morning.

SOPHIE.   Happy Birthday, Min. *(Hands her the envelope.)* This is for you.

MINNIE.   A present? This early in the day? Can I open it?

SOPHIE.   Ask Fan.

FANNIE.   Go ahead.

MINNIE.   *(Reading, but confused.)* But what does it mean?

FRANK.   It's a deed.

SOPHIE.   It's the deed to your part of this land. You're twenty-one now.

MISS LEAH.   Every colored woman ought to have a piece of land she can claim as her own.

FRANK.   Do you know how much that land is worth?

SOPHIE.   We're interested in buying more land, not selling what we've got.

FRANK.   Well, from what that white fella told me on the train, not everybody around here feels that way. I heard some of your neighbors are considering some pretty generous offers.

MISS LEAH.   Speculators!

FRANK.   They're offering $500 an acre.

MISS LEAH.   I can't believe it.

FRANK.   Doesn't that at least make you more open to the idea? You could be a very rich woman.

SOPHIE.   And I'd be standing in the middle of Kansas without any place to call home. You can't grow wheat on an acre of money.

FRANK.   There's plenty of other land around from what I could see. What's the difference?

SOPHIE.   The difference is we own this land. Whether they like it or not, and anybody who tries to say different is going to find himself buried on it.

FRANK.   You wouldn't really kill somebody over a piece of ground out in the middle of nowhere, would you?

SOPHIE.   This land is the center of the world to me as long as we're standing on it.

FRANK.   And how do you think the rest of the world feels about sharing their center with a town full of colored people?

SOPHIE.   I have no idea.

MINNIE.   None of that matters! Can't you see that none of that matters? This is the land that makes us free women, Frank. We can never sell it! Not ever! *(Wil Parrish enters and comes to the door. Fannie opens it for him.)*

FANNIE.   We thought you'd changed your mind about coming to church with us.

WIL.   On the day of Miss Sophie's speech? Not me! I'm sorry I'm late, I stopped by the telegraph office yesterday and there was a wire for Frank. *(Searches his pockets for it.)* It was too late to bring it over yesterday and this morning I forgot it, so I went back. I thought it was probably the news you been waitin' for.

FRANK.   I knew it! Didn't I tell you? I knew it! I felt our ship pulling up to the dock. Come on, Parrish! Where is the damn thing?

WIL.   Here it is. *(Frank rips it open and reads. His face hardens.)*

FRANK.   What the hell?

MINNIE. What is it? *(Frank drops the telegram on the table and walks to the bedroom, slams the door. Fannie picks up the telegram.)* Read it, Fan.

FANNIE. *(Reading.)* "Paternity denied. Stop. All claims to money, property, land and other assets of Mr. John Charles, late of New Orleans, Louisiana, denied. No legal recourse available."

MINNIE. You all go on without me. I need to ... Frank needs me here, I think.

FANNIE. All right, Baby Sister. Be strong.

MINNIE. Yes, I will. *(They exit. Minnie goes into the bedroom to Frank, who is sitting on the bed drinking from a silver flask.)* I'm so sorry!

FRANK. Are you? Sorry for what? Marrying a bastard?

MINNIE. Don't say that!

FRANK. Do you know what this means? This means I've got nothing. Not a dime. Nothing.

MINNIE. You can sell your books.

FRANK. Don't be so stupid. *(Pacing.)* They think they can make me an ordinary Negro. That's what they think. They think they're going to have a chance to treat me colored and keep me here where every ignorant white man who walks the street can make me step off to let him pass. They think they can pretend I'm nothing and — presto! — I'll be nothing.

MINNIE. You won't let them do that.

FRANK. Let them? They've done it! We don't even have passage back to London. We're stuck here being niggers. Common, ordinary, niggers!

MINNIE. It'll be all right. We don't have a lot of money, but we've got a place to live. Not forever, but just until we get on our feet. Just until the baby comes! We do have a place.

FRANK. What are you talking about?

MINNIE. We can stay here. On our own land. Right here. Until you have a chance to figure things out.

FRANK. Do you really think I could live here?

MINNIE. Sophie has plans. You'll see. It's going to be beautiful. A paradise for colored people.

FRANK. A paradise for colored people ...

MINNIE. This is our land, Frank. Nobody can take it from us. You don't have to have your father's money. We have land!

FRANK. You're right. We have land ... *(A beat.)* I'm sorry I snapped at you, darling. It's just that when I think about all the things I want to give you, it drives me crazy.

MINNIE. I love you. That's all I need.

FRANK. But you deserve so much more, Min. You're so beautiful. *(He kisses her. Touches her stomach gently.)* Did you explain to my son that his daddy has a bad temper sometimes?

MINNIE. Please try, Frank. Just try ...

FRANK. *(His mood changes abruptly.)* Don't you think I'm trying? I'm trying to be a good husband to you. And I want to be a good father. But you have to help me.

MINNIE. I need to be able to trust you again.

FRANK. You can darling. You can trust me. I swear it. I know the last few months haven't been easy, but I'll make it up to you. Do you believe me?

MINNIE. Yes, Frank ...

FRANK. It'll be just like it used to be. We'll find another place, just like the one we had before, right on the square. You liked that place, didn't you, darling?

MINNIE. It was lovely, but it costs too much money to live that way. To live abroad ...

FRANK. Your share of this land is worth over $50,000. Do you know what we can do with that kind of money in London? We'll have the best of everything and so will our baby.

MINNIE. Sophie would never sell this land to speculators. Not for a million dollars.

FRANK. It wouldn't be all of it. Just your fair share. The town is full of people looking to buy some of this land before your sister gets that damn rule passed. This is the chance we've been waiting for. A chance for me to get back on my feet. To show my brothers I don't need their money.

MINNIE. They're not your brothers. They don't even claim you!

FRANK. They don't have to claim me. I look just like them!

MINNIE. No, Frank. I can't ask Sister to split up this land.

FRANK. I'm your husband. Don't you ever tell me no! *(He reaches to grab her arm.)*
MINNIE. Don't, Frank! *(Moving quickly out of reach.)* I don't care what you do to me, but I won't let you hurt our baby!
FRANK. *(He grabs her arm and brings her up against him sharply.)* Don't you ever threaten me as long as you live, do you understand me? Do you? *(She nods silently.)* I'll kill you right now, Min. I'll break your damn neck before your precious sisters can hear you holler. I'll kill everybody in this house, don't you understand that? You want to know who I told those white men you were, Min? You really want to know? *(She struggles again, but he holds her.)* I told them you were a black whore I won in a card game. *(He laughs and presses his mouth to hers roughly.)*

BLACKOUT

Scene 3

Frank enters the main room, pulling on hat and gloves, clearly preparing to go out. Miss Leah and Fannie enter the yard. Fannie is helping Miss Leah.

FANNIE. I thought Sister's speech went well this morning, didn't you Miss Leah?
MISS LEAH. Speechifyin' and carryin' on. She ought to run for president. *(They open the door as Frank arrives at it.)*
FANNIE. Frank! You startled me.
FRANK. I'm sorry. I didn't hear you coming.
FANNIE. Are you going out?
FRANK. I won't be long. I have some business to attend to in town.
MISS LEAH. On Sunday afternoon?
FANNIE. I'm sorry about the will. I want you to know you always have a place here with us.
FRANK. Yes. Thank you. We'll figure out something.

FANNIE. Is Min going in with you?

FRANK. No, she's resting. She'll be out in a few minutes. I won't be long. *(Exits quickly.)*

FANNIE. I believe he is sorry about what happened, don't you?

MISS LEAH. A man that will hit a woman once will hit her again. *(Sophie enters and meets Frank in the yard.)*

FRANK. How was church?

SOPHIE. You should have been there. *(She crosses to the porch.)*

FRANK. You're going to have to stop being so high and mighty. It doesn't become you. *(She turns to him from the porch steps.)*

SOPHIE. I'm sorry for your troubles, because they're Min's troubles, too. But I think you should get on where you're going now and I'll go on inside.

FRANK. Well, suit yourself, as you always say, but I think I've got some news you might find interesting. *(Reaches in his pocket; Sophie shifts the gun.)* Take it easy! I'm unarmed ... as always! *(He pulls out the deed.)* I just thought you'd like to know that we're officially neighbors now. For the moment, anyway.

SOPHIE. What are you talking about?

FRANK. My wife wants me to share in her good fortune, so she's added my name to her deed.

SOPHIE. I don't believe you.

FRANK. I'd let you see it up close, but that probably isn't such a good idea. Hot-tempered woman like you ...

SOPHIE. Get off my land. You make me sick.

FRANK. I'll get off your land. I'll get so far off it the post office won't even be able to find me.

SOPHIE. That suits me fine.

FRANK. Well, maybe you'll like your new neighbors better. Ask Min about them. She met them on the train. Well, she didn't really meet them, I didn't introduce her, of course, but she saw us talking. White gentlemen. She'll remember them. She wants to tell you, but she's a little nervous about it.

SOPHIE. Tell me what?

FRANK. You can see why. You've raised her to think this place is practically holy ground. She didn't even want to talk about selling it at first, but she came around.

SOPHIE. Minnie would never sell this land. You're lying.

FRANK. Well, you let her tell you. I figured under the circumstances, I would spend the night in town. I'm sure I'll have our share sold before tomorrow. Hope the sale doesn't hurt your chances in the vote next week. *(Laughs.)* You know you're getting off easy when you think about it, Sister Sophie. I could stick around here and take over your precious town if I wanted to. You ever see a group of colored people who didn't put the lightest one in charge? *(As Frank and Sophie talk, we see Fannie and Miss Leah making coffee, starting the evening meal, etc. In the rear bedroom Minnie raises up slowly. She is obviously in great pain and has been badly beaten. She almost cannot stand. She staggers out of the bedroom. As Frank exits laughing, Minnie stumbles into the room where Miss Leah and Fannie are working.)*

MISS LEAH. Lord, chile!

FANNIE. Sister! Sister! Come quick! *(Sophie rushes into the house and runs to help.)*

BLACKOUT

Scene 4

Fannie and Wil are sitting on the porch. Wil has a shotgun.

WIL. I don't understand how a colored man can hit a colored woman, Miss Fannie. We been through too much together.

FANNIE. Maybe there's just too many memories between us.

WIL. I don't think you can have too many memories. I know I wouldn't take nothin' for none of mine.

FANNIE. Not even the bad ones?

WIL. Nope. The bad ones always make the good ones just

59

that much sweeter. *(A beat.)* Does that paper really mean Frank can sell to speculators?

FANNIE.   Well, if Baby Sister really signed it.

WIL.   I never met a colored man like Frank before. Seem like he don't care 'bout colored people no different from white folks. Miss Leah says it's because mulattos got a war in them. And sometimes it makes 'em stronger but some times it just makes 'em crazy. Makes 'em think they got a choice about if they gonna be colored or not.

FANNIE.   Sister's a mulatto and she never seems to be confused.

WIL.   Well, you're right there. *A beat.)* Miss Fannie, I want you to know ... I can take care of it.

FANNIE.   Take care of what?

WIL.   I mean, he's a colored man and I'm a colored man. We can settle it that way. Man to man.

FANNIE.   I couldn't ask you to hurt anybody.

WIL.   You can ask me to kill somebody, Miss Fannie. If I can't protect you and your sisters from a Negro who has lost his mind, what kind of man does that make me?

FANNIE.   Have you ever killed a man?

WIL.   Not a colored man, but I guess they ain't that much different from any other kind of man when you get down to it. *(We see Miss Leah and Minnie in the back. Miss Leah is holding Minnie's hand and talking directly to her.)*

MISS LEAH.   When they sold my first baby boy offa the place, I felt like I couldn't breathe for three days. After that. I could breathe a little better, but my breasts were so full of milk they'd soak the front of my dress. Overseer kept telling me he was gonna have to see if nigger milk was really chocolate like they said it was, so I had to stay away from him 'til my milk stopped runnin'. And one day I saw James and I told him they had sold the baby, but he already knew it. He had twenty been sold offa our place by that time. Never saw any of 'em.

When he told me that, I decided he was gonna at least lay eyes on at least one of his babies came through me. So next time they put us together I told him that I was gonna be sure this time he got to see his chile before Colonel Harrison sold it. But I couldn't. Not that one or the one after or the one after the ones after that. James never saw their faces. Until we got free. Then he couldn't look at 'em long enough. That was a man who loved his children. Hug 'em and kiss 'em and take 'em everywhere he go.

I think when he saw the fever take all five of them, one by one like that ... racin' each other to heaven ... it just broke him down. He'd waited so long to have his sons and now he was losing them all again. He was like a crazy man just before he died. So I buried him next to his children and I closed the door on that little piece of house we had and I started walkin' west. If I'd had wings, I'd a set out flyin' west. I needed to be some place big enough for all my sons and all my ghost grandbabies to roam around. Big enough for me to think about all that sweetness they had stole from me and James and just holler about it as loud as I want to holler.

MINNIE.   I didn't want to sign it. I was just so scared. I didn't want him to hurt the baby. I can't make him stop ... hitting me. I just ... want him ... to stop ... hitting me.

MISS LEAH.   They broke the chain, Baby Sister. But we have to build it back. And build it back strong so the next time nobody can break it. Not from the outside and not from the inside. We can't let nobody take our babies. We've given up all the babies we can afford to lose. *(A beat.)* Do you understand what I'm sayin' to you?

MINNIE.   *(Whispers.)* Yes, ma'am.

MISS LEAH.   *(Kisses her.)* Good. Go to sleep now. That baby needs a nap! *(Miss Leah goes out to Wil and Fannie.)*

FANNIE.   Is she ...

MISS LEAH.   She's sleeping. She held onto that baby, too. I told you she was stronger than you think.

FANNIE.   Thank God!

MISS LEAH.   Where is Sister?

WIL.   She wanted to be sure Frank was headed toward town and not back this way. She told me to bring you the things you wanted from the house for Miss Minnie. *(He hands her a small packet which she takes and opens carefully.)*

61

MISS LEAH. I hope she didn't forget anything.

WIL. She had it written down. *(Sophie enters on the move.)*

SOPHIE. He's on his way in, but he's moving slow. Is everything there you need?

MISS LEAH. It's here. It's here ...

SOPHIE. Min?

FANNIE. Sleeping. She's going to be okay.

SOPHIE. *(Taking charge.)* All right, here's what we're going to do. Wil, I need you to ride out and catch up with Frank. Tell him Min sent you to tell him she loves him more than anything and ... everything is going to be okay. Tell him she wants him to come here tomorrow afternoon because I'll be in town to try and stop the deal. Tell him she wants to go with him to the land office so they won't have any trouble no matter what I do.

WIL. What if he doesn't believe me? He might think it's a trick.

SOPHIE. Tell him colored men have to stick together. He'll believe you. Tell him ... tell him ... the message is from Fan. That she's on their side now. That should make him feel safe.

FANNIE. What are you going to do when he gets here?

SOPHIE. *(A beat.)* You and Miss Leah go in the back with Min.

FANNIE. But what are you going to do?

SOPHIE. A colored man who will beat a colored woman doesn't deserve to live.

FANNIE. Just like that?

SOPHIE. No. Just when he tries to kill my sister and her baby before it's even born yet!

FANNIE. Stop it! That's just what I was afraid of!

SOPHIE. What you were afraid of? Me?

FANNIE. Of what you might do.

SOPHIE. What I might do? Why aren't you afraid of what he is already doing?

FANNIE. He's her husband, Sister!

SOPHIE. If he wasn't her husband would you care what I did to him for beating her half to death?

FANNIE. That's different.

SOPHIE.   You know as well as I do there are no laws that protect a woman from her husband. Josh beat Belle for years and we all knew it. And because the sheriff didn't do anything, none of us did anything either. It wasn't a crime until he killed her! I'm not going to let that happen to Min. I'm going to watch him prance across this yard and then I'm going to step out on my front porch and blow his brains out.

FANNIE.   And then we'll be savages just like he is!

SOPHIE.   No! Then we'll be doing what free people always have to do if they're going to stay free.

FANNIE.   *(A beat.)* Isn't there any other way, Sister?

SOPHIE.   This morning, while I was standing in that church painting a picture of the future of this town, he beat her and did God knows what else to her in this house. Where she's always been safe. We can't let him do that, Fan. All the dreams we have for Nicodemus, all the churches and schools and libraries we can build don't mean a thing if a colored woman isn't safe in her own house. *(Fannie turns away.)*

WIL.   *(Quickly.)* You don't have to do this. I already told Miss Fannie. All you have to do is say the word.

SOPHIE.   What are you talking about?

WIL.   I can take care of it. You can wait here with your sisters and I'll take care of everything.

SOPHIE.   I appreciate the offer, but the day I need somebody else to defend my land and my family is the day *that* somebody's name will be on the deed. I need you to help me do what needs to be done. Not do it for me.

WIL.   You can count on me.

SOPHIE.   Good! Go on now. I don't want him to get too far ahead of you.

WIL.   I'll catch him. *(Exits.)*

MISS LEAH.   I can't let you do this.

SOPHIE.   I'm not asking you. This is something I have to do.

MISS LEAH.   And why is that? Because he hit your baby sister or because he wants to sell your land to some white folks?

SOPHIE.   Aren't those reasons good enough for you?

MISS LEAH.   Where's the pie tin? *(She gets up and starts lay-*

63

ing out utensils, ingredients, etc. to make a pie. This activity goes on throughout the following dialogue.)

SOPHIE. What?

MISS LEAH. The pie tin.

FANNIE. It's in the cupboard. What are you doing?

MISS LEAH. We're going to make an apple pie.

SOPHIE. An apple pie?

MISS LEAH. In case you forgot, this is still the state of Kansas, a part of the United States of America. Men beat their wives every day of the week, includin' Sunday, and white folks cheat colored folks every time they get a mind to.

SOPHIE. I know all that.

MISS LEAH. Good. I remember when y'all first got here. Green as you could be. Even you, Sister Sophie, way back then. Your group was as raggedy as any we'd seen. All of y'all lookin' like somethin' the cat dragged in. And then here come Min, bouncin' off the back of your wagon, hair all over her head, big ol' eyes and just the sweetest lil' face I ever saw. Didn't even known enough to be scared. *(A beat.)* Hand me the sugar.

FANNIE. Are you feeling all right?

MISS LEAH. Am I feelin' all right? If I was you, I'd be worried about folks talkin' 'bout shootin' somebody. That's who I'd be worryin' about. It's a messy business, shootin' folks. It ain't like killing a hog, you know. Sheriff has to come. White folks have to come. All that come with shootin' somebody.

But folks die all kinds of ways. Sometimes they be goin' along just as nice as you please and they heart just give out. Just like that. Don't nobody know why. Things just happen. *(A beat.)* One day a little bit before I left the plantation, Colonel Harrison bought him a new cook. Ella. She was a big strong woman. She didn't make no trouble either. Just worked hard and kept to herself. Ella knew a lot about herbs. What to put in to make it taste good. Colonel Harrison just love the way she cook. He used to let her roam all over the plantation pickin' wild herbs to put in her soups and stews. And she wouldn't tell nobody what she use. Said it was secrets from Africa. White folks didn't need to know. Colonel Harrison just laugh. He was eatin' good and didn't care 'bout where it come from no way. But after awhile, that overseer started messin' around her. Tryin' to get Colonel Harrison to let him have his way with her, but Colonel Harrison said no and told him to stay from around her. She belonged in the kitchen. But that ol' overseer still wanted her and everybody knew next time he had a chance, he was gonna get her.

So one day, Colonel Harrison went to town. Gonna be gone all day. So that overseer put some poor colored man in charge of our misery and walked on up to the house like he was the master now 'cause Colonel Harrison gone off for the day. And when he walk up on the back porch, he had one thing on his mind, but Ella had been up early too, and the first thing he saw before he even saw her was a fresh apple pie coolin' in the window. And it smelled so good, he almost forgot what he come for. And Ella opened the screen door and smile like he the person she wanna see most in this world and she ask him if he'd like a glass of cold milk and a piece of her hot apple pie. Of course he did! What man wouldn't? And he sat down there and she cut him a big ol' piece and she told him it was hot and to be careful not to burn hisself.... And do you know what happened? Well, he didn't even get to finish that piece of pie Ella cut for him so pretty. Heart just stopped right in the middle of a great big bite. By the time the master got back, they had him laid out in the barn and Ella was long gone. *(A beat.)* But she did do one last thing before she left.
FANNIE.   And what was that?
MISS LEAH.   She gave me her recipe for apple pie.

BLACKOUT

Scene 5

Miss Leah is in the back sitting with Minnie who is lying down. Sophie and Wil are hiding outside. Fannie is alone in the kitchen where she checks the time and then goes to the oven and takes out a perfect pie.

Frank enters the yard furtively. Fannie sees him and watches him from the window. She takes off her apron and goes to the door. She opens it before he knocks. He steps back, startled.

FANNIE.   Come in, Frank. *(Frank hesitates.)* Sister's gone to town and Miss Leah's in the back with Min. Please. Come in.

FRANK.   Parrish said you were going to come into the land office with me. Are you ready?

FANNIE.   It's all right. Sister isn't angry anymore. She wants to make you an offer.

FRANK.   What kind of offer?

FANNIE.   Please. Come inside so we can talk.

FRANK.   I don't want any trouble.

FANNIE.   We're prepared to make you an offer for your land.

FRANK.   You can't afford what they're paying in town.

FANNIE.   We're prepared to pay exactly what they're paying in town.

FRANK.   You don't have that kind of money. Minnie said so.

FANNIE.   Sister and I didn't involve Min in all the details of our household finances. I'll go into town with you now and we can make all arrangements. Do you have the deed? *(Franks shows it and puts it back in his pocket.)* Good!

FRANK.   That's fine by me. I don't care where the money comes from as long as it ends up in my pocket so I can get the hell out of this place! *(Extends his hand.)* Can we seal the deal, Fannie? Just the two of us?

FANNIE.   Done.

FRANK.   You know I'm sorry it had to go this far in the first place. I love Minnie ... how is she?

FANNIE. She's asleep right now. Miss Leah's with her.

FRANK. Good, good.

FANNIE. She wanted me to wake her up as soon as you got here, but I told her to get a few more minutes rest and I'd give you a piece of homemade apple pie to keep you busy in the meantime.

FRANK. You're not angry with me? About Min, I mean. You know how aggravating she can be sometimes. She's such a child.

FANNIE. I understand. She has to understand that a wife's first allegiance is to her husband.

FRANK. Well, you're a very understanding person and I appreciate that, but I would just as soon we get on our way. I don't think your sister would be too happy to come home and find me sitting at her table eating up all her ...

FANNIE. *(Holding out a piece to him.)* ... apple pie. My specialty. Sister won't be home for hours yet. Besides, now that we know we'll be able to keep the land in the family, Sister's not one to hold a grudge.

FRANK. I don't know about that. She didn't seem to mind swinging that shotgun my direction.

FANNIE. We've got to put all that behind us now. For Min's sake and for the sake of your baby. I know Sister's prepared to let bygones be bygones. In fact, when she saw me rolling out the crust for this pie, she told me to make sure you got a piece of it.

FRANK. She did? Well, it takes a better man than I am to refuse an invitation for a piece of your famous apple pie! *(He sits and begins to eat heartily.)* Delicious! Well, you tell Sophie she's not going to have to worry about Frank Charles hanging around getting in her hair. Not me! *(Laughs, coughs a little.)* Soon as I get everything signed and proper, good-bye Niggerdemus! Hello London! They treat me like a human being over there. You wouldn't believe it. Half the people we know don't even know I'm colored. I told Min if she was just a couple of shades lighter, we could travel first class all over the world. Nobody would suspect a thing. *(Laughs, coughs a little, loosens his tie.)* Don't get me wrong. I don't outright pass.

67

I just let people draw their own conclusions. *(Coughs harder as Fannie watches impassively.)* Can you get me a glass of water, please? I feel a little ... strange.

FANNIE.   No, Frank. I can't do that.

FRANK.   Please! I ... water ... my throat's on fire! *(He suddenly realizes.)* What have you done? My god, help me! Please help me! *(She watches him as he tries to stand, but can't. He looks at her in a panic, then slumps over: dead. Fannie shudders slightly: it's over. She composes herself, goes to the door and waves a signal to Sophie and Wil who come immediately. Wil checks the body to be sure Frank is dead. He nods to Sophie and they begin gathering Frank's things to remove the body. Minnie and Miss Leah, hearing the activity, enter from the back. Minnie moves slowly from her injuries and from her reluctance to see the result of their collective action. They see that Frank is dead. Miss Leah watches Minnie who moves toward the body then stops, looking at Frank with a mixture of regret and relief. She approaches the body slowly, her anger and fear battling her bittersweet memories of the love she once felt for Frank. She reaches out and touches him tentatively, realizing the enormity of what they have done. She draws back, but reaches out again, almost involuntarily, to touch his arm, his hand, his shoulder. We see her move through a complex set of emotions, ending with her knowledge of the monster Frank had become. Her face now shows her resolve and even her body seems to gain strength. She steels herself and reaches into Frank's pocket to withdraw the deed. She clutches it in her hand then looks to Sophie, who stands watching her. Minnie takes a step toward Sophie and extends the deed to her in anticipation of Sophie demanding the return of the deed. Instead, Sophie re-closes Minnie's hand around the deed and gently pushes Minnie's hand with the deed back to her. Minnie, grateful and relieved and finally safe, clutches the deed to her chest with both hands.)*

BLACKOUT

Scene 6

Miss Leah is sleeping in her chair at the table. The cradle is on the table and one of her hands touches it protectively. Minnie enters from the back, dressed for the dance in town. She stops and looks at Miss Leah and her baby. She does not go to them, but looks for a minute and then around the room, slowly. She walks past the side board, touching it absently. She walks to the door and stands looking out at the full moon. She absently touches the broach at her throat. Her hair is braided with ribbons and she wears bright clothes. She looks calm and healthy. She feels Miss Leah's eyes on her and turns. They share a look. Both smile slowly.

MINNIE.   It's as bright as noon out there.

MISS LEAH.   That's a good luck moon. It's gonna be a good day tomorrow.

MINNIE.   Do you think so?

MISS LEAH.   It's gonna be a good day every day.

MINNIE.   How do I look?

MISS LEAH.   You look beautiful, Baby Sister.

MINNIE.   Is she sleeping? Look! Her eyes are wide open! Hello, darling!

MISS LEAH.   She's thinkin'.

MINNIE.   *(Crooning to the baby.)* What can my sweet baby be thinking, huh? What are you thinking about?

MISS LEAH.   Leave the chile in peace now! Everybody's got a right to their own thoughts.

MINNIE.   Do you think she's warm enough?

MISS LEAH.   You're gonna smother the child if you're not careful. It's spring! Time to let some air get to her.

MINNIE.   I know. I even took my shawl off while I was hanging clothes out today.

MISS LEAH.   You better stop that foolishness! This is still pneumonia weather!

MINNIE.   You just said winter was over, Miss Leah.

MISS LEAH.   Well, it'll be back before you know it. *(Fannie and Sophie enter from the back. Fannie is dressed up and Sophie has on a severe dark blue dress.)*
FANNIE.   How do we look? *(She twirls around happily.)*
MINNIE.   You look wonderful! Wil Parrish will be beside himself to have such a beautiful fiancé!
SOPHIE.   If colored people paid as much attention to saving the race as they do to their dancing, we'd be free by now.
FANNIE.   Oh, hush! It's been so peaceful around here since you pushed that vote on through and the speculators went home, it's time to do a little dancing!
MINNIE.   You're too plain, Sister.
SOPHIE.   Too plain! This is my best dress!
MINNIE.   It needs ... something. Here! *(She takes the broach from her own bodice, kisses it, and pins it on Sophie.)* It's Mama's! Don't lose it!
SOPHIE.   I'll guard it with my life! *(Wil enters the yard. He carries flowers.)*
FANNIE.   He's right on time! *(She opens the door happily.)* Good evening, Wil.
WIL.   And to you, Fannie. These are for you. Hello, Miss Leah. Everybody.
MISS LEAH.   Please get these women out of here. They are drivin' my granddaughter crazy with all their chatterin'!
MINNIE.   We're going! We're going! Are you sure she'll be okay? I can stay here with ...
MISS LEAH.   I'm not so old I can't handle one little baby! Go on and leave us some peace.
WIL.   Baker and his Mrs. passed me on their way!
SOPHIE.   They didn't have that bad baby with them, did they?
MISS LEAH.   You know that girl don't go no place without carryin' that big head boy with 'em.
FANNIE.   He's not that bad!
SOPHIE.   Bad enough! *(Fussing with the pin.)* Go on! Go on! I'm coming. *(Fussing with the pin.)* Go on! I'm coming.
MINNIE, FANNIE and WIL.   Good night. *(Etc. They exit.)*
SOPHIE.   Too plain! That girl will have me looking like a

Christmas tree if I'm not careful.

MISS LEAH.   You look fine.

SOPHIE.   Thank you.

MISS LEAH.   Now don't you go makin' any speeches tonight! This is a dance.

SOPHIE.   I won't, Miss Leah. Not tonight.

MISS LEAH.   Go on, now!

SOPHIE.   *(Putting the gun beside Miss Leah's chair.)* We won't be too late. *(Sophie exits to the yard. As Miss Leah talks, Sophie walks into the middle of the yard and looks up at the full moon. She extends her arms and slowly turns around to encompass her land, her freedom, the moon, her life and the life of her sisters. She is completely at peace. Miss Leah reaches into the cradle and gently lifts the well wrapped baby out and looks into her face.)*

MISS LEAH.   Yes, my granddaughter. We got plenty to talk about, me and you. I'm going to tell you about your momma and her momma and her gran'momma before that one. All those strong colored women makin' a way for little ol' you. Yes, they did! 'Cause they knew you were comin'. And wadn't nobody gonna keep you from us. Not my granddaughter! Yes, yes, yes! All those fine colored women, makin' a place for you. And I'm gonna tell you all about 'em. Yes, I sure am. I surely am ... *(As Miss Leah rocks the baby, crooning softly to her, Sophie continues to spin slowly in the moonlight as the lights fade to black.)*

END OF PLAY

PROPERTY LIST

KITCHEN
5 serving bowls
1 chicken platter
Black biscuit plate with biscuits
Blue/black coffee cup
Silver ladle
Black pie pan
3 plain napkins
3 soup spoons
2 teaspoons
3 serving spoons
6 wrapped sets of silverware
6 dinner plates
5 dessert plates
2 cups and saucers
6 wine glasses
Desert plate
1 fork
1 small paring knife
Brown mixing bowl
Match boxes with matches
Food: greens, potatoes, stew
Coffee pot
Stew pot
Brass tea kettle
Silver pie spatula
Sweet potato pie
Wooden spoon
2 pot holders
Red water pitcher
Iron kettle
Plate
Small iron

Crockery
Utensils
Cloth
Ladle
Soup bowls
Jar of tomatoes
Sugar bowl
Bowl of apples
2 towels on hooks
Flour canister
Sugar canister
Coffee canister
Tea Canister
Coffee cup
Hanging peppers
Red wood bowl
Wooden gun box
Brown bottle
Small rag
Weighted string with wood
2 gun shells
Box of gun shells
Apple pie tin
2 tins
11 canning jars
Woven basket
Coffee grinder
Rolling pin
Brown bowl
Large wash tub with small basin inside
Towels
Wicker baskets
Crock canister
Crock jug
Washboard
Gray enamel bowl
Small broom
Slop bucket

Tinder box with wood and fire poker
Brass basket (hanging)
3 cast iron pots (hanging)
Large iron skillet (hanging)
Small iron skillet (hanging)

MAIN ROOM
Cloth runner for dining room table
Bible
Wooden box
Green vase with flowers
2 brass framed photos
Knitted covering for round table
Silver framed photo
Cloth runner for sideboard
1 candlestick with candle
Loose matches (in candlesticks)
Oil lamp (practical)
Glass vase (empty)
3 water glasses
Crystal water pitcher
Square small ceramic vase
Brown ashtray with pipe
Box of matches
Green blanket for trunk
Apron on wall hook
Green shawl on hook
Blue shawl on hook

ON SIDEBOARD
4 serving spoons
3 plain napkins
3 soup spoons
1 teaspoon
6 sets of silverware
Salt and pepper shakers

6 wine glasses
Coffee cup and saucer
6 dinner plates
5 dessert plates

DESK
Candlestick with candle
Loose matches
Ashtray
4 boxes of matches
Eyeglasses with case (FANNIE)
Journal (FANNIE)
Ink well with ink
Handkerchief (SOPHIE)
3 sharp pencils
Map of Nicodemus with ribbon (SOPHIE)
Blank paper
Letters
Ledger (SOPHIE)
Book (FANNIE)

BEDROOM
Quilt on bed
2 pillows on bed
Cedar chest with:
       brush
       small black comb
       hand mirror
       cigar (unwrapped)
       small black book
3 books
2 framed photos

OUTSIDE
Yellow flower in hole
Wood pile (8 small pieces)
1 tree stump
1/2 log
Clothesline with a bag of clothes pins
3 towels on clothesline
Washtub
Washboard
Bark

SR PROP TABLE PRESET
Basket with flowers (yellow hues)
Purple flower in basket (WIL)
Loaded gun (SOPHIE)
Sack of sugar
Grocery sack with:
> oatmeal
> coffee
> paper bag
> string licorice
> tobacco pouch with tobacco

3 letters
Small blue envelope with deed
Gun (WIL)
Flask with water
Box of matches
Shawl (FANNIE)

UC PROP TABLE PRESET
Sewing basket with:
> darning sock with needle
> bloomers with needle
> thimble

Coffee cup

Written speech
Apple pie
Spatula with wood handle
Dessert plate
Fork
Plain napkins
Cigar
Bottle of red wine
Extra slop bucket liner
Cutting board
Parsley
Knife
Table cloth
Large brown comb
2 blue and white hair ribbons
Cup and saucer with:
       cheese cloth
       loose tea
Bowl of oatmeal
Teaspoon
Cradle
Baby with wrap
1 set red roses
Small brown bag with:
       bottle of liquid
       bark

DSL PROP TABLE PRESET
Telegram in envelope
Suitcase
Small poetry book
Cigar
Box of matches
Axe
1/2 log

1 set flowers (daisies)
1 set flowers (wild flowers)
1 set flowers (small roses and white flowers)

PERSONAL — PRESET
Cigar (FRANK)
Box of matches (FRANK)
Pocket knife (WIL)
Sharpening stone (WIL)

SOUND EFFECTS

Train whistle

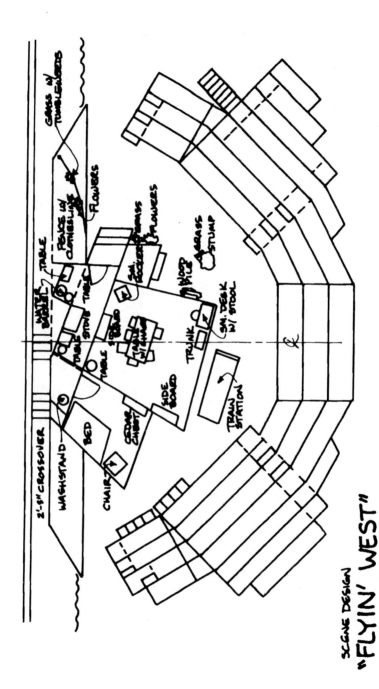

SCENE DESIGN
"FLYIN' WEST"
(DESIGNED BY DEX EDWARDS FOR ALLIANCE THEATRE COMPANY)